The Corporate Ladder

The Corporate Ladder

How to stay away from the Corporate Career Trap?

Roberto Villalvazo

Copyright © 2023 by Roberto Villalvazo
Printed in the United States of America

ISBN-10: 1977889719
ISBN-13: 978-1977889713

All rights reserved. This book or any portion thereof may not be reproduced or used in any manner without the author's express written permission except for using brief quotations in a book review.

DISCLAIMER AND LEGAL NOTICE: The information presented herein presents the author's view as of the publication date. Because of the rate with which conditions change, the author reserves the right to alter and update his opinion based on new information or any other condition. This book is for reference, informational and inspiring purposes only. The author's opinion expressed in this book is not trying to tell the reader what they should do or implement in their organizations. Every effort has been made to accurately represent the contents presented here.

I dedicate this book to my sons, who are my greatest inspiration source.

CONTENTS

Introduction		xi
Chapter 1	Finding your Place	1
Chapter 2	Organizational Evolution vs. Personal Stages	31
Chapter 3	Personal Growth	51
Chapter 4	Growth-based Career Culture	77
Chapter 5	Unleash your Potential	99
Chapter 6	The Evolution of Work	117
Chapter 7	The New Normal & The Great Resignation in the World	139
Acknowledgments		145
About the Author		149

INTRODUCTION

For years, the corporate career models pointed us in the direction where moving up the corporate ladder matters, even if we do not fully understand what that means or why that is important.

Sometimes, the aspiration is not in sync with reality, and nobody takes the time to mentor or help us to realign our priorities and aspirations. Only a few leaders ask us what we want "To Do" in their career dialogues when trying to guide us to find our path. The problem worsens because HR folks and managers generally cannot elaborate on a career conversation based on meaningful experiences and the type of work we would like to do. Usually, the discussions are around promotions and which will be the next positions.

In recent years, career models have been evolving, partly because of the pandemic but also for the new economic challenges and to better fit the new generations' expectations.

Despite these challenges, traditional career development models propose growth as a map of interconnected positions that follow a sequence in time where the growth typically goes up in the organizational hierarchy. That approach focuses on positions, and promotion-based growth encourages the "To Be" thinking in the people and within the organization's culture. Nowadays, many companies consider that approach unsustainable and unreal. Instead, the new career development approaches evolved into something more dynamic based on growing through gaining experiences and applying knowledge where the skills and interests drive people's growth. So then, the new game is not about the role but skills and learning experiences.

It is crucial to understand and learn how organizations evolve and the different stages where an organization goes over time, including the competencies required at each stage to take ownership of our development and align our expectations.

In 2016, I met Julie Winkle, co-author of the book, "*Help Them Grow or Watch Them Go.*" After attending her sessions, I understood the difference between focusing my career conversation on the "To Do" instead of "To Be," which changed my thinking and perspective about career development and progression.

Today, I am not focused on my next position or promotion. Instead, I started looking for valuable experiences that helped me reach my potential and continue growing as a person and leader. To explain the shift from focusing on the "To Be" to "To Do," we need to go back in time and remember when we were children or adolescents. I am sure many of you have heard at least several times about the importance of being the best in whatever you do or needing to succeed in a corporate environment.

Unfortunately, that approach somehow programmed our brain to think the way where the

"To Be" and superficial aspects are the central points of your thoughts and actions.

To reflect on that, let's think about how many times you or somebody else told you phrases like the following:

- What do you want <u>to be</u>?
- You never will <u>make enough money</u> in that career!
- <u>Be the best</u> to progress in your career.
- Need to <u>follow the steps of your parents</u>.
- I want <u>to be</u> the next CEO.
- I would like to <u>have that office</u>.

I heard those phrases from different people in my life. Also, I told them too often in my infancy and adulthood that I programmed myself to play the same game. However, all those statements have something in common: they focus on material, superficial aspects or gaining status. So this is one of the reasons I decided to write this book because I also grew up with those paradigms.

Nowadays, when I think about all those phrases I have heard for years, it sounds as if everything I learned about career progression is related to superficial matters, and as well as many people, I played that game too.

I remember competing about status with colleagues in my office and people outside my workplace by convincing me that I needed to be the best; I wanted to be the expert. I felt that gaining that status would help me escalate the corporate ladder faster. Now, I recognize that I was wrong and invested too much time and effort into pursuing the incorrect goal in my development.

When I changed my mindset about the purpose of career progression, I understood that I was feeding my ego, trying to demonstrate that I deserved more than others under the excuse of being the best in my area of expertise. The problem is that we forget to enjoy what we do because we are too busy trying to be something and competing with others.

Once we are in that trap, we do not take the

time to stop and think about what we like to do to be happy. Instead, we spend too much time and energy pleasing others that we forget to focus on our passions and be in balance. Sometimes we are willing to sacrifice essential things in our lives that will never come back, like time with family, friends, or ourselves. Indeed, time is one of our more precious resources, so use it wisely.

Another example that demonstrates that we have been thinking of being something or someone is when you were a student and got enrolled in a career or program. At that moment in your life, what influenced your decision? Did someone explain what it is about being an engineer, accountant, salesperson, technician, or any other profession in the real world? Do you know what type of work you will perform in the following years? What information did you have when you finished the studies that helped validate if your aspiration matches the reality? And more important, did somebody talk to or mentor you to validate if you would be happy doing that? Is that what will help you to be in balance and unleash your potential?

Most of the answers to those questions and the information we had that guided our decision was founded on the style of thinking we learned in infancy and adolescence, where we try to be someone. Frequently some years later, we discovered our choice did not match our reality or passions. In my case, I thought it was pretty clear that I wanted to be an engineer, but after two years of working in IT, I decided to move to Human Resources because I enjoyed better what I did there. If this is your situation, I invite you to take the time to reflect on what you want to DO instead of what you want to BE to have more clarity on which path you want to follow. If you take the time to think about what makes you happy, you will better know which direction could be better for you.

The next question is whether your thinking aligns more with the "To Be" style or the "To Do." You can discover that by listening to your first words when introducing yourself. For example, do you start your introduction by saying your work title? If that is your case, it is possible that your thinking is more aligned toward "To Be." You can start rewiring your brain by saying, "Hello, my name is Robert, and I work at Company XYZ in Human Resources.

As you can observe in the example, we focus our answer not on the "nobiliary" title but on who we are as individuals. We learned that the title gives us prestige. Avoid starting with the title when introducing yourself because you reinforce the To Be, not the To Do. If you have kids, I invite you to begin teaching them to think about what they want to DO. Again, the challenge is to start thinking more about what we want to DO to enjoy our careers and life. The question is if we will be able to shift that mindset. So, how can we start thinking about the "to DO" to enjoy our careers instead of seeking the following position or title? We will talk about this in the following chapters. Part of enjoying the journey is being in flow. Chapter 3 will cover what being in flow means for us and our career development. I will also explain the importance of understanding human capability as part of our nature and how it relates to our career development and aspirations.

When we understand the connections between human capability and development, we can maximize our potential to do things that fulfill us. There is a connection between being in flow with the feeling of happiness or being overwhelmed that matches our human capability, allowing us to deal with the complexity and how we perceive things. I have been working with career development and learning topics for over twenty years, but I have learned more in the last ten years, reflecting on that connection. I have been curious to understand those concepts and their relationship with career development.

I changed my understanding of career development and progression when I understood those concepts. As a result, I find myself on a continuous journey of seeking valuable career experience that matters to me. Learning about these concepts guided me to understand better the dynamics of the employee's life cycle within the organizations and how we can align better with our aspirations. It is interesting how by using these concepts, we can better understand some of the changes and decisions we made in our lives and the aspects driving us toward the future.

In Chapter 2, we will address topics related to creative thinking and personal stages, among other aspects related. Then, in Chapter 6, which I hope complements your vision around career development and future challenges, we will talk about the evolution of work.

By the end of the book, you will probably see career development differently. You will be able to value how powerful it could be if you change your paradigms related to career progression by just shifting the focus of your conversations.

I am sure that with the references presented in the book, you will make a better decision in your career and life. For some people, career growth means climbing the corporate ladder. They see career progression as a race where you need to go up as fast as possible and use career progression as the vehicle to feed your egos. Instead, I see career development and progression as an opportunity to align our aspirations with our capability to be in flow. In that journey, we must constantly recalibrate our path to align with our passions and interests. Then, when we look back, the journey should be something that we feel joy and pride of what we did.

Sometimes we must stop and change our lenses to find the answers and refocus. Unfortunately, some people never find the answer to their questions or prefer to live avoiding them. Other people spend their professional careers looking for the ideal job, position, or company when everything is inside of them.

Ultimately, the question is what career development means to you and what makes you happy. This book of reference invites you to reflect on what career development means, identifying the moments that matter in your life to be happy and live in harmony. When you read the book, I hope a new mindset sparks inside you to generate well-being in society.

For the organizations, I invite them to contribute by offering better experiences and conditions to whom collaborate with them because the big resignation is about rebalancing priorities. It is time to disrupt ourselves and seek new forms that drive the history of humanity.

It is time to align and balance the organization's interests and individuals' aspirations for a better society. We are living new realities that allow us to try new ways of development and growth. If we do not start thinking more collectively as human beings, it will not be a future for anyone. So, step away from the corporate ladder trap to enjoy a new way of thinking about career progression and work-life balance to pursue happiness.

I hope you enjoy the book!

Roberto Villalvazo

CHAPTER 1

FINDING YOUR PLACE

The Individual Contribution

It was the autumn of 2005 when I arrived in Washington, DC, to start working for one of the multilateral organizations with Headquarters nearby the White House. For the first time, I was working full-time outside Mexico and was ready for a new beginning.

I remember many emotions going through my mind the first day I arrived at my new office. When I was waiting in the lobby, I felt like I had been there for an eternity until someone appeared to show me where I should go. After all, I was too anxious to demonstrate what I could do and learn about my new job that I felt I couldn't wait any longer.

At the end of my first day, I returned to my apartment in Georgetown with a big smile. That evening, I spent some time lien on my bed, assimilating the new environment and imagining what would come in the following days. I was overexcited and full of energy.

During my first weeks, everything was new, and I enjoyed every moment of that new experience. I didn't know at that point how different it would be to work for a multilateral organization which differed significantly from what I had learned in previous jobs. However, I was confident in myself and had all the attitude and energy to demonstrate my capabilities from the beginning. I thought I had unique skills that could give me some advantages over other colleagues who had been there for many years, but that idea will play against me in the mid-time. When I reflect on that thinking, I understand that the problem was that I did not understand the organizational culture and environment. That blindness drove me into frustrations and internal conversations trying to deal with the new situations.

At first, I was unsure about my role or what I would do in the following years. I felt nobody cared except me, which generated frustration because I perceived my work as very basic. My initial job was to prepare Excel spreadsheets and templates in Microsoft Word to document competencies. Honestly, I was in shock because I had a managerial role in my previous company, and now I was formatting spreadsheets in Excel.

To help you picture the work environment, most people there had at least 20 to 25 years of tenure, and many never worked elsewhere. In addition, most young people started their careers as interns doing paperwork or working on formatting documents, so that duty was pretty standard. Maybe that is why nobody expected me to demonstrate anything in the short term; ultimately, I will have plenty of time to show my abilities. Since I came from outside, I didn't get it because I came from an environment that taught me to rush in my career, so it took me time to assimilate.

After some years, I understood that I was the one that didn't fit into that environment, at least not at the beginning. But, to be fair, I must say that not everything was as terrible as it sounded.

My colleagues and Boss were excellent, and almost everyone was very kind. I had the privilege of having a pretty office on the 4th floor next to the corner where I could see President Obama's caravan every time he went out. Also, I could see the snow falling during the winter and the people and some tourists hanging out in summer.

One day, our assistant approached me to check if I was ok. She told me I was pushing too hard on myself and suggested to slow down and relax a bit. She was right because moving to a new country involves a lot of changes that take time to adjust. So, the truth is that all the people around me understood what was happening except me. They were so kind and willing to help me adapt that sometimes it could be overwhelming.

During my time in DC, I met incredible people. Some were relatives of influential people involved in politics in their countries or had senior positions in their previous companies. It surprised me that they were humble and preferred a low profile. I learned a lot from all of them, personally and professionally speaking.

The Boss

My Boss, a couple of years older than me, was very knowledgeable and upbeat, and even when I disagreed with him in many cases because of his style, I recognized his experience. As my leader, he was very committed to making me feel appreciated and welcome from the first day. He gave me his full support since day one.

He is one of the best HR professionals I have ever met in my professional life. Before joining the Organization, he was an entrepreneur, so he had a strong sense of pleasing internal clients and trying to be perfect in our work. This drove us to spend long hours at the office trying to finish everything perfectly. I remember we worked until 2 am many days and stopped just because I told him I needed to go and sleep.

He always wanted to be the best, so he was constantly reading, doing research, or thinking about contributing to the Organization's agenda. He was always looking for what else we could do and frequently said that we could not afford to make mistakes. We invested too many hours just trying to improve the quality of the work a little bit that it felt not worth it. He often mentioned that our work must be perfect because most of what we did have high visibility to the Senior Leadership and the Board of Directors, so there was no room for errors.

During my time in HR, we were the only team that worked that amount of hours, except for the advisor of General Manager, who also worked very hard and could keep the whole Department busy when she needed something. One of her responsibilities was to produce a monthly booklet with people's demographics. We didn't have a system or dashboard to support the process in those days, so most of the work was manual. That implicates much time reviewing the data, graphics, colors, and wording before it was ok. Sometimes, it took us the entire week, and many people just looked for any error in the document. As I mentioned, the document needed to be perfect.

The interest think is that not everyone could work on that. It was a selective team, so you needed to be invited by the team to perform that work because if you were not in the core team, you couldn't work on it. That might sound silly, but that's how it worked since it was founded on trust, hard work, and quality. So to get invited, that team needs to perceive you as a hard worker.

As you can imagine, my luck and charisma drag me into that adventure quite early. Maybe the team regretted it later because I challenged if that work should be performed manually or needed to be automated, allowing us better use of our time and skills in something else.

At that point, I am pretty sure that my Boss noticed my anxiety and observed how I struggled to appreciate the value of our work in the Organization's context. He dedicated time daily to help me understand the culture and how those small things matter. He shared his experiences from arriving at the Organization and how he learned the culture. One morning he came into my office to share one of his stories about how somebody approached him and asked him not to participate too much in the meetings unless The Boss asked for his opinion. After that, he told me:

"Remember, we are here to make The Boss shine. If The Boss shines, we will shine too."

In a certain way, he was trying to tell me that he also felt underused and frustrated. Then, the following week, we were talking about our future in DC when he said:

"We are not here to make a career. The people that work here are the best and have brilliant careers. Most of them had good positions before coming here. We are here to use our knowledge and experience to contribute to the mission of the Organization."

To hear something like that was pretty shocking for someone who did not understand what he was trying to say. In part, because it was a misalign between his words and my aspirations but also because I could not see the importance of learning the cultural style and playing the political game as others. I was not interested in learning about the importance of the organization's forms or my Boss's stories.

When I finally realized what he told me, it did not take me too long to understand the importance of finding a place in an organization. Some weeks later, I learned another lesson, but this time, it came from another person who was the Unit Chief of the Department. He was a brilliant guy from Argentina who was one of my first friends and later one of the toughest people I needed to deal with whenever I presented something.

He could challenge whatever you say, but despite that, I respect him and frequently ask for his opinion and advice because he makes me think. He was like an uncomfortable mentor since he was a pain.

In a certain way, he helped me improve my skills to defend my proposals with solid arguments and a clear understanding of the "why" of my recommendations. He was one of the most challenging guys that I had ever met.

When I needed to present my work to the top management, I always showed my slides and ideas to him. He usually replayed with the same question. Ok, but why? He didn't stop asking questions until you demonstrated solid arguments and good thinking of what you were saying.

I remember some of his questions:

Why do we need to do that?
Why that approach and not another?
What are the benefits?
How would you guarantee the results?

I wouldn't say I liked that little game since he enjoyed putting me on the spot, but I learned a lot from him. Those questions always forced me to go back to the board and prepare better my arguments to support my recommendations. The good news for me was that he had an unfair reputation for always being against everything, so people avoided arguing with him or listening to his comments, except me. Somehow, it was a safe place to argue because even if he strongly disagreed with my opinion, nobody would take the time to consider his objections. For me, it was an excellent way to improve my presentations. So in a certain way, it was a perfect safe school for me.

Now, I recognize that thanks to him, who pushed my thinking style too hard, I have reached my potential and adopted a working style that still helps me whenever I propose something. Without notice, he taught me to defend my points using arguments that resonated with the senior management rather than just using concepts or answering as a technical expert.

At that moment, I changed the direction of my career and my interests to focus on different aspects. I was no longer interested in being an expert or recognized for my expertise and knowledge. Other people helped me understand the Organization and find my place, so eventually, I got it. I was surrounded by amazing people willing to share their journey with me, like the Boss of the Argentinian guy who one day called

Finding your Place

me to give me some advice. Of course, my first reaction was, "Damn it, another one is giving me advice! And I thought, what does this guy want? Why suddenly does everyone want to advise me? The truth is that without knowing, his advice will be one of the most valuable that anyone could give me in years.

Once at his office, instead of talking about my work, he started with some casual conversation until he abruptly stopped and said: "You need to find your place," and he added, "it should be something that nobody is doing, but you can do." When you find it take that place as yours. In the meanwhile, try to help others.

Then, he said, "You are a smart guy just you do not understand the game yet." At that moment, I thought, "Oh my God! Where am I working?" So, I thought, now this guy who doesn't know anything about me tells me I need to find my place. So, what is that stuff of finding my place? I asked myself. I did not recognize him as someone who could help or advise me. He had been working there for many years, and I did not appreciate the value of his advice.

That day, when I went home to have dinner with my wife, I shared, as many other times, what just happened that day and how that guy approached me with all that crap as if he understood what I was feeling or thinking. But, of course, she was smart and immediately understood what was going on, so she just listened and said: "well, you do not lose anything by listening, right?" I didn't pay much attention to her comment, but it took me some days to comprehend the situation and her words.

In the following weeks, the guy did not mention anything. It was as if we had never had that conversation. Then, one morning, he stopped by my office and asked me: "So, did you find your place?"

After working in that Organization for maybe 30 years, it was evident to him that something was happening to me and that I did not understand the situation. I am sure he could smell my anxiety from miles. It was as if I was the only one who maybe didn't notice or refused to accept what was happening, so I replied to him: "Well, no! Not yet, but I am working on it". The truth was that I did not have a clue about where to start. Finally, he told me, "Fine, just let me know if you want to talk about it or have any questions," He left my office.

The next day, I went to his office and invited him to a cup of coffee in the cafeteria. Initially, we discussed generic topics such as the weather, my car, family, and DC until we finally addressed the matter. I told him, "I think you know I am not happy because I can do more than just Excel files, checking formulas, reports, and things like that, but I do not know how to demonstrate that." Then, after a short pause, he looked at me and asked: "Does your Boss appreciate that work? Do your Boss trust and support you?" Can anyone in the Department do what you are doing?" But maybe the most crucial question he asked was, "Did the big Boss value your work and involved you in his projects?" Of course, he was not expecting an answer because he already knew the answers to those questions. However, it was evident that my aspirations were misaligned with what the team needed for me.

After that, he told me, "You know that very few people have access to The Boss, right? Even some people who have been here for many years have never met him yet or gotten involved in his projects, and you, in a short time, got his attention, and he invited you to his core team because he values your work and trusts you. So, why is it too important for you if that work is basic?" Then smiling, he said, "I think you found your place on this team, be smart, and have patience because that will be the beginning." For the first time since I arrived, I felt I understood the game and the purpose of my role. Finally, I put my ego in second place and opened my mind. That simple contribution allowed me to do more complex tasks and take on leadership roles on other responsibilities.

Some takeaways that I would like to share are:

- Before trying to fly, take your time to learn about the culture and the Organization.
- Listen to all the comments from people trying to help you, regardless of who it is or which position they have.
- Sometimes, little contributions will open bigger doors.
- Be humble to show your greatness. Put your ego aside.
- Open your eyes to new opportunities.
- Take time to pause, reflect and change your lenses.
- What you have learned maybe is what is not allowing you to grow. Learn to let things go!
- Your past will help you to understand your present but will not necessarily help you to build your future.

The Next Move

Some months later, from my conversation about finding my place and understanding how to grow in the Organization, I started thinking about my next move. I felt I could offer other experience and knowledge even though they valued my technical skills.

The challenge was about how to get involved in other projects without losing anything I have gained, including my position and visibility in the team. So, now in my head, the question was how to find a way to demonstrate that I can do more and participate in or lead new projects.

I knew that my Boss and his Boss put a high value on my job, not because they thought it was too complex but because I was doing something nobody else couldn't do then. So that taught me that work does not necessarily need to be complex to be meaningful and appreciated by the Organization. So with this in mind, we can say that in some cases, the perceived value will depend on the value and interest others put into our work.

We tend to think more complex work will accelerate career movements, which is not necessarily true. Sometimes it is not the right moment to pursue a career move. If that is the case, let's work on preparing the environments to make it happens. The pauses in our development allow us to align our aspirations with the environment. It is possible that in most cases when we feel frustrated with our career's progression, our expectations and ego are involved. My discomfort was not with the work itself; it was more about my ego and job expectations. My lack of understanding of the Organization and unwillingness to appreciate and see the value of my work made me think that I deserved a better assignment when that assignment had high value for the team. I was looking outside me when the answer was always inside me but hidden by my ego.

Finally, I understood that my simple work would be the key to achieving bigger goals and happiness. With this understanding, I want to exemplify why it is essential to understand your real purpose.

It is not the short term that will give you happiness and satisfaction. It is not what you do that matters but why you do it, and the value of your work makes the difference.

As Jones Dewitt, a former photographer for National Geographic, once said, "sometimes you only need to refocus." In other words, you must change your lenses to see different perspectives and find your goal because your vision is unclear.

Looking for the Right Experiences

Finding the right experiences is not always easy or natural. Sometimes, we have opportunities in front of us, and we do not notice them. Many factors can blind your sight while pursuing the right experience for you. Remember that good experiences are something subjective that will change over time. Not only because of the context change and your aspirations but also because you will evolve no matter what you do. Your potential and capability will not be the same today as tomorrow. You will give different values and will see things differently over time.

Learning how to find your place in the Organization is essential, but also it is imperative to decide what you want to do and which are the right experiences for you. Remember to clear your vision, think about why you want to do it, and then put all your passion into achieving it.

To find the right experience, you need to be selective since you do not want to be involved in every project that will distract you and not allow you to plan your next move. Someone once told me,

"Be present and absent at your convenience," and "Do not be so useful that people use you."

In reality, the right experience for you is the one that helps you to keep learning and moving with purpose. The experience is the Why, not the How, so follow your dreams, define goals, and do not hesitate to change your path if that is not the best for you.

Finding your Purpose

Do you ask yourself why you work? What are your motivations for waking up every morning to do whatever you do? Which will be your legacy when you die? We must stop and reflect on these questions at some point in our lives.

The first time someone asked me those questions was in 2000 when I was driving back home. Suddenly the person next to me, who later became my wife, asked me about my purpose in life and how I imagined my future.

I was unprepared for those questions since I never stopped thinking about them. I was never interested in slowing down and thinking about my future until that day.

Since then, I have never forgotten her questions because it was so spontaneous but profound at the same time. In a certain way, her words are still present every time I decide what to do with my life. That is an example of how a simple question can transform our lives if we stop, think, and reflect on it. That day when she asked, "How do you want to transcend in your life?" she made me think about what I have been doing all these years.

Sometimes those questions could scare us, but it is worth it. I was petrified, without knowing what to say, trying to find the correct answer, but the truth is that there are no right or wrong answers. That day, I was speechless, so I just looked at her, and with a smile, I continued driving. It was clear that I did not have a clue or know what to say because I had never in my life been worried about that.

Later that day, and quite joking, I thought, "well, if I became a superhero right now, my main power would be….hmm, maybe be breathing." It might sound funny, but it was just an example of how I lived without purpose. As of that day, I was achieving superficial "success."

I was conscious for some minutes that I was following a routine without direction. I was like the little boat in the lake, moving and swinging with the wind. It took me almost 15 years to consciously define my life and work drivers. Maybe my vision and passion were fuzzy enough that I could not see my path.

For almost fifty years, only three people asked me questions like that, my ex-wife, my friend Lotfi and a young lady who invited me to a job interview in 2018. Three persons in 50 years! As you can see, very few people will ask you questions like that, so the questions need to come from you.

Once, a person asked me, "What was my life philosophy?" So, I hope you can see why you need to find people who make you think and grow because very few will ask you questions that make you think and reflect on what matters.

The book "Finding your Why" talks about some steps to finding your purpose and how you can identify what you need to modify to be better. The author mentioned, "Happiness comes from what we do and Fulfillment from why we do it."

As I mentioned, knowing what you want to Do and why will be crucial in your journey to find your place and happiness.

Work-Life-Balance and Passions

Some years ago, a colleague researching Work-Life-Balance asked me if I considered a difference in what people valued depending on their generation. I answered that, in my opinion, it is not about generational preferences but about connecting with their passions and interests. I think that part of the challenge is more related to the feeling of losing or gaining something.

Many of us refer to or make work-life balance decisions with the mindset of a trade-off, which should not be like that. Yet, somehow, the pandemic shows us that work-life balance is more about learning how to connect better with all aspects of our life equally.

When we do a decision thinking that implicates losing something, then at some point, it will be a feeling of regret. The same happens in our personal relationships as in our working ones. If we are not in balance and feel that it is fair, we will feel frustrated, disappointed, or incomplete at some point. Therefore, we need to learn how to compaginated all together in a limited timeframe that allows us to rest, recreate ourselves and learn to keep moving forward as human beings. Then, it is not about what the Organization can provide us (food, funny furniture, video games, etc.) or if people work long or short hours. It is about how people feel and connect. If people do not feel happy doing their job or in the environment, they will sooner or later leave. So then, I asked you this question: "Do you know anyone living their dreams and/or very connected with their passions to quit or give up? Or complaining? Do you know people who feel in balance complain that it is sacrificing something or think they should be doing other stuff? I observed that regardless of the amount of effort, time, and difficulties that implicate or demand doing something, if people are in flow, they are willing to do more.

In my opinion, the big resignation, which is a complex issue, is partly related to feeling good. The absence of that feeling impacts people, and they are willing to change their priorities because they feel disconnected from other aspects of their lives or feel that the trade-off is not good enough to continue in that pattern.

I define work-life balance as the exchange of effort multiplied by the time invested to achieve a result that transforms into the individual's happiness.

Then
>if the effort in terms of Time Invested is bigger than Happiness, then people will quit or leave,

also
>if the effort in terms of Time Invested is smaller than happiness, then people will stay, and they will be proactive, even giving a discretionary effort,

but
>if effort in terms of Time Invested equals happiness, people will just do their work and leave as soon as possible.

You can associate this with the level of engagement and passion. Following the same rationale, we should seek experiences that make us happy. Think about if what you do is related to what makes you happy and your purpose because it is the only way your work will not be "Just a Job."

Finally, think about why you are doing what you are doing. For example, some people ask for or accept jobs because they want visibility, but for what purpose? Remember that visibility will not give you recognition; it will not necessarily give you visibility nor make you happy.

Change your mindset to break the pattern of sacrificing something to get something else and learn how to put in balance all the pieces of your life.

Small things can open big doors.

CHAPTER 2

ORGANIZATIONAL EVOLUTION VS. PERSONAL STAGES

I learned to understand the different organization's stages and evolution during my professional career. I understood that aligning our expectations and aspirations with the organization's challenges is critical to maximizing our contributions. If you can not read the corporate environment and understand how your organization is evolving, you may be unable to re-align your development plan when those changes happen. I observed that we can align our development with the organizational stages if we know what is more appreciated by the organization at each stage and align with their priorities.

To explain that better, let me refer to the Ichak Adizes Corporate Lifecycle model that addresses the organizations' challenges when organizations evolve and become more mature and move to the next level of complexity.

It is essential to understand the differences at each stage and what the organizations need to focus on to understand which experiences and competencies we need to pursue. If you learn to identify those elements, it will be easier for you to direct your development in that direction to focus on the capabilities, competencies, and skills that will be more appreciated by the organization and by yourself. Also, it will help you decide what organization is a better fit for you so you can plan your next move better or seek the right experiences to help you keep growing.

Adizes named the first five stages of his model as Infancy, Go-Go, Adolescence, Prime, and Stable. His model has four more stages we will not cover in this book, but as a reference, those are Aristocrat, Early Bureaucracy, Bureaucracy, and

Death.

Let's focus on the first five stages. You can learn more about Adizes' model in his book "The Corporate Life-cycle." In addition, we have to consider the human aspects. Therefore, I will refer to some elements of Dr. Elliott Jaques's work included in his Requisite Organization model, which will help us address that aspect.

By learning about his concepts, you can understand what is required at each organizational level, the nature of work, and the complexity involved in the organizations in a time span then you can make the connection towards your development. Also, you will see what is the most important for the organization based on the nature of the work and how you can add value.

To start practicing and connecting the dots, I will show in the next chapter some examples where I will correlate the complexity required with learning experiences and competencies using something Elliott developed called the potential progression curves.

In general terms, the potential progression curves show the transition of our human capability in the time-life as part of our nature.

Elliott's model helps to understand what organizations require to succeed at each stage of their evolution by identifying the nature of the work and its complexity. To explain that, he used the concepts of strata, like in geology, to explain the complexity and nature involved in each organizational layer. Each stratum refers to a type of work that must be performed to contribute to the success of any organization.

There are many books where Dr. Elliott Jaques explains his model in detail, such as in "The Requisite Organization," where you can find more information about his model. In this book, I will make some references and connections to his work and show you how I made the connections for my own development. Learning to identify your connections could be a game changer when you think about your development and the relevant aspects of your life.

Understanding the Company Transitions

As I mentioned, something that is extremely valuable for your development is learning to identify the different momentums and transitions of the organizations. By understanding the nature of work at each stage, you can focus your development better and acquire the right skills. Also, your contributions will be more meaningful, and you will be aligned with the organization. You can also extrapolate that to your function or work and observe how long your organization or work takes to transition to the next stage to keep the focus on what is relevant. Also, observing if the transition is linear or in cycles and the risks and opportunities during the journey will be vital.

In this regard, understanding how fast a company moves among stages could be vital in deciding which organization is better for you. It is common to observe organizations in the early stages move very fast. They have accelerated peaks (up and down) versus a more mature organization where its transitions are more steady at taking more time going in circles until they achieve the next stage.

We could think about this in the context of the business areas or the corporate functions by reflecting on how an HR function change compared to Finance. You may perceive Finance as more linear and steady, with minor transitions in nature, profiles, and skills.

In comparison, if we could imagine the corporate function of Human Resources in terms of a line, we will probably see its evolution more like waves over time but more like a belt curve when it does not have transitions. Of course, this is not a rule, but I use the analogy to explain how it is a way that you can think and reflect on the nature and evolution of the functions in the organization to decide when it is time to move to your next challenge.

Understanding the Personal Transitions

I mentioned Elliott Jaques several times, so maybe you will ask yourself, "Who the Hell is Elliott Jaques?" Those were the exact words that Jerry Harvey asked himself when he heard about him.

Elliott Jaques is perhaps the most brilliant management scientist on the planet. He was a clinical psychiatrist who worked with corporations in addition to seeing patients. He dedicated 55 years of his life to continuous research. Elliott Jaques wrote many books and was a research professor at George Washington University. He graduated with an MD from Johns Hopkins University and received a Ph.D. in social relations from Harvard University as many other credentials.

Elliott Jaques is also known as the originator of concepts such as corporate culture, midlife crisis, fair pay, maturation curves, the time span of discretion, and requisite organization as a total system of managerial organization. Peter Drucker called his work "the most extensive study of actual worker behavior in the large-scale industry."

Now that you know the importance of Elliott's contribution to this field, let me start by mentioning that we all have a particular human capability that is part of our DNA. It is part of our nature and can't be naturally modified or changed, and it grows over the years just because we are alive. That nature determines our maximum capability and how we can deal with the complexity in a time span to make decisions and solve problems using our discretionary judgment. We can nurture that capability to achieve our maximum potential and capability by choosing the right learning experiences that help us grow and apply our capability to fulfill our potential.

When we apply our capability, we have a certain level of interest and passion in doing it, and when we acquire the skills, we have some level of engagement with the experience to achieve it. This connects with something I will cover in the following chapters: the four absolutes to succeed in any role.

Elliott defined in his model different strata to identify attributes, trails, and natures associated with each layer. Reviewing the potential progression curves shows that some curves cross different strata in time, and the lower curve remains in the same strata. That is because there is a group whose human capability remains steady over time at that stratum compared to others moving across different strata within the same curve during its evolution. Usually, the lower level curves are related to work whose nature is to produce and ensure the production gets done. It is essential to mention that there are no better or worst strata. All the strata are equally important and play a crucial role in the organizations. I will focus more on the first five strata and how those connect with your development from a practitioner's perspective. I will also share a theoretical model that could help you to define a learning journey for anyone since its onboarding.

To move on to the next topic, you need to know the nature of the work associated with each stratum. Then we will connect with the organizational transitions using the model of the Corporate Lifecycles of Ichak Adizes.

The first five stratum levels of Elliot Jaques are related to the following contribution to the organization:

Level 1: Production
Level 2: Make sure production gets done
Level 3: Create, improve, and monitor systems
Level 4: Integrate multiple systems
Level 5: Creates a strategic vision

If your human capability evolves within a curve that crosses different levels, then you must plan your journey in that direction and identify what is important for your future. In addition, you will need to determine what you need to master and which skills are just transitory because they will be used temporarily to round your profile.

Connecting Company Evolution, Nature of Work, and Personal Development

When we learn to identify the main attributes of the organizations at their different stage of evolution, it will be easier to align our development and interest. The two models I previously mentioned can help you understand at which moment your organization or any other organization you could be interested in.

As you might remember, the first stage in the corporate lifecycle model is called Infancy. At that stage, the organization is focused on earning money. In other words, the focus is the sales and having products or services to sell. Even though the people working in the organization will be friends and family at this stage, the nature of the work is to get productions done. That type of work matches level 1 in Elliott's model.

If you work in an organization at the Infancy stage, the most appreciated contribution will be your skills and abilities to produce a product or deliver the service.

Many new companies fail at the first stage, but if they survive, they need to focus on the next stage, shift their focus to established methods that will help them with consistency, and start building the sustainability required at the next stage. Remember that a steady evolution requires bringing predictability into the organization's growth.

It will be highly appreciated if you work for an organization at this stage to learn about best practices and gain deep knowledge. If you are in the stage of your personal development where you want to be an expert, then organization at this stage and next could be the best fit for you. The main difference between the organizations at the Go-Go and Adolescence stages is their focus.

At the Go-Go stage, the focus is on incorporating best practices, documenting processes, and things that will help them establish a form or work, reducing the overlapping of functions and tasks. In addition, as in the previous stage, you will seek some efficiencies.

Organizational vs. Personal Stages

At the Adolescence stage, the focus is more on integrating the different functions and systems at the time that tries to improve the effectiveness and profits. If your organization is at this stage, then learning about follow-up, planning, and controlling tools and methods could be the best way to add value to your organization, even though some of those skills could be transitory in your journey.

Most people will work in these kinds of organizations, and their human capability and interest will align more with these stages and levels. You can do the same exercise for the following two levels considering that you will need another thinking style to deal with the complexity. I will cover these in Chapter 4. However, it is crucial to remember that if there is a mismatch between the person and the nature of the work or the organization's stage, it is possible that the person feels that they do not fit.

Transform Individual Value into Organizational Value

We can add value to the organization in different ways. For example, I observed that if we understand the evolution of the work in the various functions, we will be more aware of the cycles in the organization and predict when our job could be perceived as less relevant or redundant.

To explain this better, let's use an example of an HR function that started as a department mainly focused on the transaction of their processes. Now, as part of its strategic vision wants to become a strategic function in the next five years. To do that, the HR department will evolve through different stages similar to the organizations and must decide what is more important at each stage.

Also, it will be essential to recognize the nature of the work at each stage and the type of leaders and employees you need to support the

Organizational vs. Personal Stages

transformation. But, of course, as you can imagine, the HR function will go through the same stages mentioned in the Corporate Lifecycle.

In this example, in year one, the function is highly focused on providing a service and offering tools to manage some processes. The nature of the work will be at levels 1 and 2 in Elliott's model, where the tasks are repetitive, and the contributions more appreciated are related to the operational knowledge base on following procedures and policies or your knowledge of operating a system.

At this stage, the primary purpose is to produce (for example, execute processes or deliver a service to our clients). The expertise required involves using tools to do the work and people solving problems by trial and error. We also ensure the production gets done, so we need tools to monitor and follow up on the implementation using checklists, meetings, etc., to help us perform the function's duties.

When the focus is on the transaction, it is not rare to observe that leaders use the authority of their role to control the execution of the function. The gap in seniority is based on the experience managing the processes more than other aspects. Since work is a commodity at this stage, the gap will be closed at some point, and then we could have a conflict if the people working in the function can deal with more complexity.

In year two, the natural next step in the transformation journey of the function is to start building and integrating the systems to support the organizational growth and function's evolution. It is time to deal with some organizational behaviors and add value differently. Knowledge per se is not the most important, but what you can do with it. The value of the transaction itself passes to the second plain of importance, and now we need to add value by advising the organization and guiding other leaders. To do it, we will use tools for planning, diagrams to explain to the organization, metrics, etc. We will solve problems and add value not only with best practices but also with root cause analysis and seeking efficiency and function effectiveness. The leaders of the function will need to be more willing to collaborate with others and have a parallel thing to anticipate issues and mitigate adverse situations that attempt towards the evolution of the function.

This stage is the foundation of the following stages, and many cultural aspects will be touched upon. Here is where we could find a more considerable resistance to the change, which is natural, so your value-added should be with expertise and a vision and understanding of a bigger picture to make the connection and project them into the next 3-5 years.

Creativity, resiliency, and persistence will be tested at this stage. Most of the transformation processes fail at this stage to rush things, so take the time to allow the organization to digest the changes and prepare for the next stage.

In the following years, focusing on maturing what you have achieved so far is critical to face what in Adize's model is called the Prime and Stable stages. During that time, you must add value by proposing improvements, monitoring, and consolidating what you built.

Once you get there, you will need to start thinking of a new cycle as part of the evolution of the function. We add value differently at each stage of the journey. There will be moments when we will not be in flow or even where our work is less relevant, but by understanding this now, you can anticipate yourself and find a way to continue contributing to the process.

Always think about the nature of the work that is your compass. It will guide your decisions and actions. Similar roles could have different levels of complexity and expected contributions depending on their nature, so they require other profiles.

Be prepared to deal with a lack of understanding from the people in the organization that, in theory, should know the nature of the roles, but the reality is other.

In this regard, I will share with you a story, one day, I asked a recruiter to explain me the expected contribution of an open role of Quality Manager that had been posted for a while, and she said, "it is about quality."

We do not need to be genius to know that, right? But, of course, it is not enough to know that it is about quality because there could be many ways a Quality Manager contributes. The problem is that many people do not really understand the purpose and nature of the work and then choose the wrong people for that job. So, in the example, that position could be related to just monitoring the quality, or it could be about creating a culture of quality where inclusively need to consider safety processes, or it could be related to improving the quality and redesigning process, training, etc. So, all of those are valid but have different natures, complexity, and scope and require different people to succeed. In other words, the required capability differs depending on the work's nature.

CHAPTER 3

PERSONAL GROWTH

Be in Flow

Being in flow is an essential part of our personal growth. As described by psychologist Mihaly Csikszentmihalyi, we are in a state of 'flow' when the challenge of what there is to do is in balance with what we feel capable of doing.

When a person is "In-Flow," there is a sense of well-being and harmony. Usually, when someone is in flow, our interest and passion will be more visible, and our engagement will increase. On the contrary, when the work's complexity exceeds the person's human capability, they can feel anxiety, perplexity, or apprehension. Another situation we could observe is that the person works long hours, which in some cases could be misunderstood as commitment and be rewarded by a leader when the challenge is bigger than the person's capability.

The opposite situation happens when the complexity is too low versus the human capability of the person; then this could feel frustration, boredom, or in some cases, the person over-complicates things just because they can do it.

States of Thinking

By understanding the different states of thinking, we can learn how our minds process information and seek learning activities that best fit our thinking states. As the state of thinking is dynamic and related to our human capability, it occurs at a specific time.

If we use Elliott's model, we will find that people at stratum 1 have a state of thinking that he called declarative because it is sustained on an opinion without too much support that it is right or wrong. In that state of thinking, things are black or white. This makes sense if we remember that a person in stratum 1 has a problems solving method based on trial and error. For people with declarative thinking, we must provide learning experiences where they can learn by doing. They cannot connect the dots, so the information should be straightforward.

The next "state of thinking" is founded on identifying patterns by accumulating information that eventually brings a solution. This state of thinking he called cumulative because it gathers information at the time of processing the data. In Boolean logic, it will be associated with the "AND." The best fit to learn if you are in this state of thinking is by studying manuals, learning about good practices, or any other documented information.

In Elliott's model, serial thinking is the following state of thinking associated with people at stratum 3. This state of thinking uses logic to identify cause-effect answers. The best learning experiences for this state of thinking maybe are activities that use cases or require connecting some dots to find the solution. In Boolean logic, this state of thinking is related to the command "IF...THEN," which clearly shows a relationship between the variables or situations.

Lastly, we have parallel thinking. This state of thinking can handle multiple scenarios at the same time and make connections to analyze a problem or situation, identifying dependencies and independencies. If we relate that with the

Boolean command, it should be related to "IF…AND…ONLY…IF". There are not many learning experiences, so maybe on-the-job training with the support of mentors or a shadow buddy could be an excellent way to learn if you are in this state of thinking. Also, simulations, scenario analysis, or playing with hypotheses could bring good learning opportunities.

Decision-Making and Problem-Solving

The states of thinking are directly related to how we solve problems and make a decision. For example, some people solve problems using trial and error methods; others can deal with more complexity and ambiguity or use methods to analyze market trends. Using the strata, we observe that Decision-Making and Problem-Solving are linked to our human capability.

In the following table, you can see which Problem-Solving is used at each Strata level.

Strata (S)	Problem Solving
S V	Market Analysis
S IV	Systems Analysis
S III	Root Cause Analysis
S II	Best Practices, Documented Experiences
S I	Trial & Error

There are big debates about if problem-solving and decision-making are different or if within the decision process is implicit the problem-solving process, which in that case, we could consider both to be the same.

In their research, D'Zurilla and Chang defined problem-solving as the logical search for a solution through applying skills and techniques designed to maximize the probability of finding the "best" or most flexible solution for a particular problem. If logical reasoning is considered one of the most fundamental cognitive activities, the definition of D'Zurilla and Chang aligns with Elliott's approach.

Aside from the debate, according to Elliott's work, problem-solving and decision-making are somehow associated with our cognitive part. Therefore, it is essential to know that people in the upper strata can use different problem-solving methods related to lower strata but not the other way around. Keep that in mind if you are in a managerial role or providing learning solutions.

Connect Capability to Development

Now that we understand the different attributes of the stratum, we will associate them with a mix of learning experiences that can help us to plan our development. With this approach, we can give transparency and certainty to anyone in our organization.

Next, I will show you a learning triangle that exemplifies the connection between learning experiences and potential progression curves. Although the learning triangle focuses on skills, competencies, and experience, it is essential to know that judgment plays a crucial role when complexity and uncertainty increase. So, we can say that skills, knowledge, and experience are enough for decision-making in normal conditions, but we need to rely on judgment in more complex situations. Then if judgment is an essential piece of the puzzle, we need to understand what judgment is. A definition of judgment is the mental ability to understand something, form an

Personal Growth

opinion, and reach a decision.

Since individual capability is not enough, we must consider additional elements such as knowledge, skills, experience, critical behaviors, and judgement to reach our maximum potential.

To connect capability to development, I developed something that I called the learning triangle. The learning triangle is a simplified representation that combines technical skills in one axe and people skills in the other. Both are necessary for our careers, but what change in time and level is the mix of both. There are two additional elements that complement its structure, as I will show you below: the Levels and Segments.

The levels and segments will help us to play with the breadth and depth of the skills and competencies in the context of the expected contribution and eventually will guide us to define the mix of skills required at each level.

Once the triangle is determined, the last part is to map it with the stratum, as I will show you. Of course, each company can define the mix of skills differently, but generally, it can be used in any organization according to the specific levels of contribution expected.

This approach is based on defining the organizational level's contributions which are the nature of work rather than positions or roles, which give us more flexibility and certainty across time and matches better with a career model based on growth by experiences.

Building and Use the Learning Triangle

To define the Learning Triangle, we will use the concepts that we have learned related to stratum, expected contribution by organizational level (nature of work), problem-solving, and tools used on each level. So, I will explain the mental process step by step using abstract concepts that you will need to replace with the accurate data of your organization. In other words, it will be like a mathematical equation where you only need to replace the variables with data. So let's begin!

Step 1: In this step, you must understand the expected contribution of your roles at each organizational layer regardless of the function.

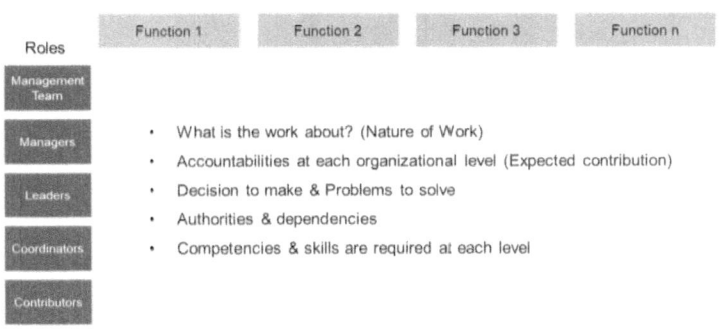

Step 2: Identify by organizational level the People skills, Technical Skills, Competencies, and experiences required to succeed at each level. Use the nature of work concepts as a guideline to decide which skills are critical at each level, regardless of the function. Remember that our driver is the nature of the work and the expected contribution at each organizational layer.

As shown in the image below, you can draw the learning triangle first and add your role levels on the left side to validate your skills and their mix.

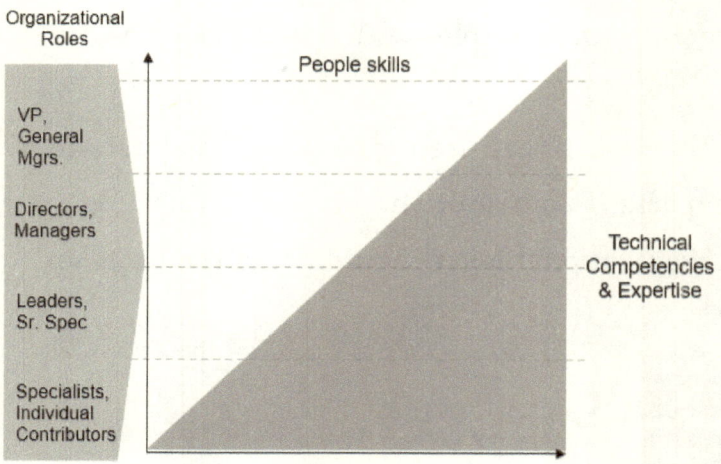

Then you will fill the triangle with the most critical skills required to succeed at each level. As you can observe, lower levels of the triangle predominate Technical Competencies, Skills, and Experiences, but it is the opposite at the upper levels. Therefore, as a guideline, you can define the mix of skills as follow: (considering 4 levels)

Level	People Skill	Technical Skill
Level 1	20%	80%
Level 2	40%	60%
Level 3	60%	40%
Level 4	80%	20%

Once you define the mix of skills by level (see table above), now you will populate the table. For representation purposes, I will use letters and numbers to exemplify how they will be used in the following steps. For example, I will use letters in the image below to represent development activities associated with technical competencies, skills, and experiences.

The numbers in the triangle represent the development activities related to People skills. Remember, this is just an example. To use the model, you must replace letters and numbers with your development activities and the organizational roles, which are there for a demonstrative purpose.

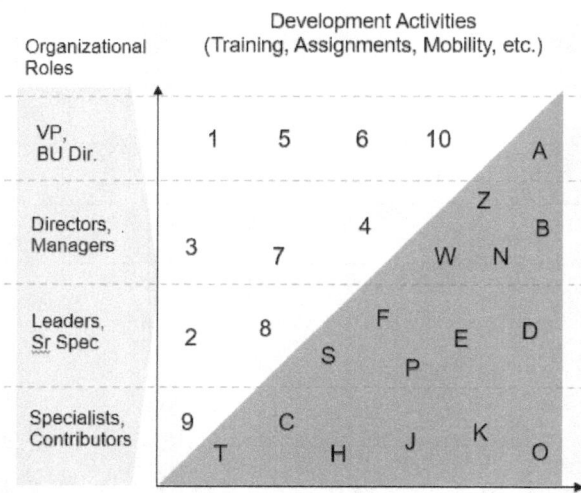

As shown in the image above, the distribution of the development activities follows the percentages proposed in the previous table.

Personal Growth

Let's see how we could map the triangle with the potential progression curves. Although, as seen in the image below, the curves match our organizational roles.

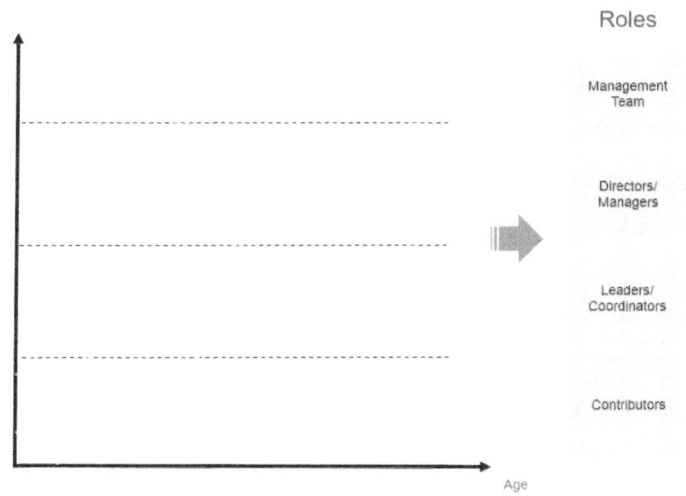

The people transitioning along the curves must go through different strata over the years until they reach their maximum capability at the end of their professional life. Remember that people grow along the curves and never can jump from one curve to another because it is our DNA. Therefore, it is crucial to understand how people transition over the years and what will be the end since some skills will be transitory during the journey. Also, by understanding the curves, we can see that some careers will be more steady and focus on technical aspects while others will be more accelerated.

The same approach works when you need to decide which is the next position or level in your development and if that one will be transitory or if you will make a career there.

The curves are an essential tool when planning talent development and pools. However, to use them properly, you must get certified to avoid misinterpretations, and the mapping of people within the curves should be done by experts in the methodology. There is a company called Bioss based in London that is an expert in managing and designing these tools and advising companies on how to use them as a competitive advantage.

If you do not want to use the curves, you can apply the model using the organizational levels of your learning triangle. You will test potential by continuously observing the applied capability by assigning more complex challenges every time to your key talent and documenting the results.

To explain the following steps, I will reference the potential progression curves and the learning triangle to cover both scenarios. By integrating the two parts of the equation, I can project a possible career path with a multidirectional approach depending on my passions and interests over time.

I can do the same without having the curves, but it will require more conversations that validate the person's capability with their aspiration and will be less visual.

Planning our Learning Journey

We must be aware of our capabilities, passions, and interests to plan our learning journey. That understanding will allow us to know: What we want to pursue versus what we should pursue at some specific time. It is essential to understand that because sometimes what we have in mind differs from what we should seek to reach our maximum potential.

In the same way, we need to understand and be aware of what we like, can, or should do because each could point us in very different directions, and not necessarily all are the best for us. The other aspect we need to understand is that learning journeys consist of multiple experiences that will help us develop and reach our potential.

In many cases, people think about the experiences as the "why" when it is just the vehicle ("How"). So, with that in mind, and now that we defined the development activities in our learning triangle, let's see how we can use them to develop a career development plan.

The first step is to honestly introspect about our passions and interests and determine what type of work we are passionate about. Now, think about what you want to do in five years and reflect on how difficult it could be for you to do that, where your gaps are, and if you really feel capable of enjoying that job. Then, with that personal exercise, you will start figuring out how to project your development over the next 5 to 10 years. Finally, please talk with your manager about it, be open to receiving feedback, and listen to others' opinions about how they perceive your capability to work together on your development plan and future opportunities.

Remember that a development journey requires you to partner with your manager and others to reach your potential. Using the learning triangle, you or the organization can help you plan your development by segments where you could have clarity over time.

Let's take as an example a person currently at stratum III, in their late-20s, and has the potential to perform a senior executive role if it reaches its potential. In addition, its interest and passions point in that direction. So, the question is how to support its development using the learning triangle.

I will not use the curves this time since most of you will not use that approach, so let's see how we can do it. Instead of the curves, I will use the segments (SE) and levels directly in the triangle, as I explained before, to define career development sections over time, as shown in the following image.

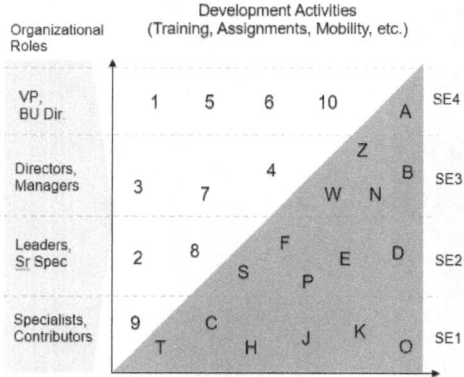

Now that I have identified the segments on the right side of the triangle, I will imagine the

Personal Growth

natural projection of the person over time to reach that level and how fast it should be transitioning to achieve it.

Next, I want to show you how it will look if you use curves. That will give us visual help to follow the explanation.

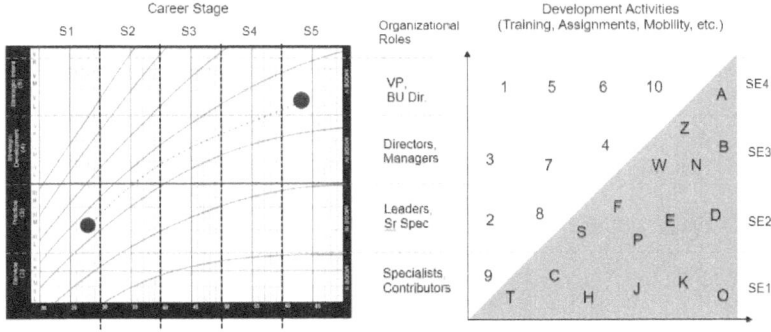

As you can see in the previous image, the person transitions over the same curve crossing the segments SE2. SE3 and ends at SE4. So, we will use those segments to build a proposed career development plan.

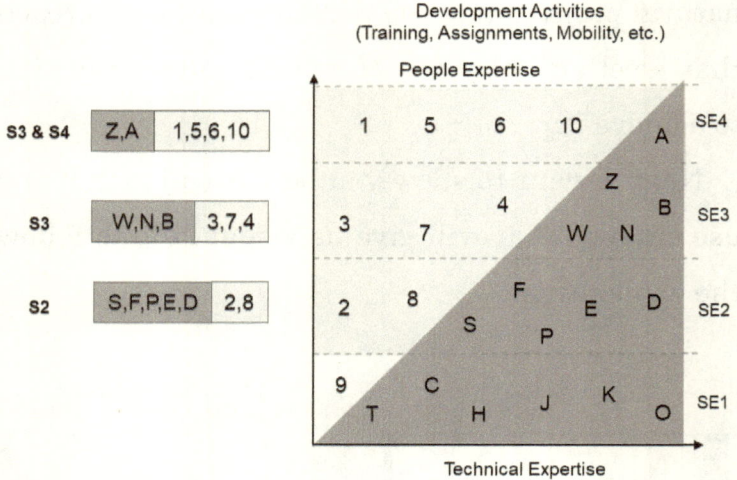

If you are not using the curves, then build the development action plan considering only not more than two segments. In other words, do not project too far through the organizational layers; you must adjust your strategy every two years based on the person's potential. Also, you will need to guess how fast it will take for the person to transition from one organizational layer to another and how much of each segment is required. When we use the curves, the transition in years is there, so it is easier. For example, in the previous case, the person is 28 yrs old. As shown in the curve, transitioning from SE2 to SE3 will take the person around 5 to 7 years, which makes sense since transitioning from a specialist, or an expert, to a managerial role takes time until you mature other competencies and you make the switch.

Then it will be in SE3 for 10 to 15 years, developing and reaching its potential to finally reach SE4 at the end of the person's career, which in terms of development could be another 5 to 7 years, depending on the person.

As you notice, we built a development plan using a mix of learning experiences for the next 20 to 25 years, but since it is not linear, the development plan should be reviewed and adjusted over time.

We need to consider that at some point, a person could take a break or gain more expertise in a specific area, as I will show you next to incorporate that scenario into the model using the scope, breadth, and depth.

Scope, Breadth, and Depth

When defining the development plan, if the person wants to specialize in a topic, we need to make it explicit in the development plan, as shown below.

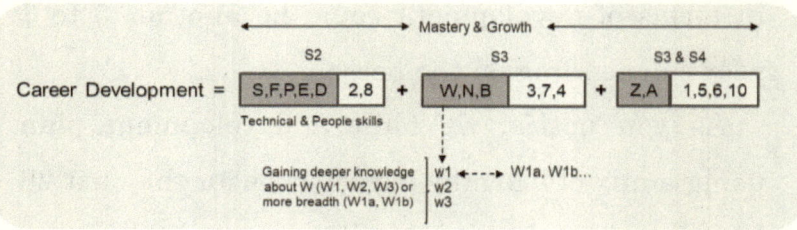

It is important to define when the person could be ready to move to the subsequent development plan segment by explaining each segment's expected minimum completion percentage.

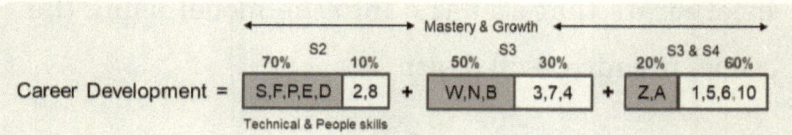

We need to constantly calibrate the plan and expectations through development dialogues to offer a positive development experience to the person.

CHAPTER 4

GROWTH-BASED CAREER CULTURE

Talk about growth-based career culture is to talk about experiences and moving in different directions. In recent years, companies have started moving toward this approach since they can't longer support promotion-based cultures in addition that are unrealistic, and most employees are dissatisfied with future career opportunities in their organizations.

Some benefits of the growth-based career model are that it increases employee engagement, career partnerships, internal mobility (employability), and the visibility of career opportunities impacting attraction and hiring cost reductions.

According to Garner in their study "The New Path Forward," 46% of transitioning leaders underperform during the transition, as shown in the image.

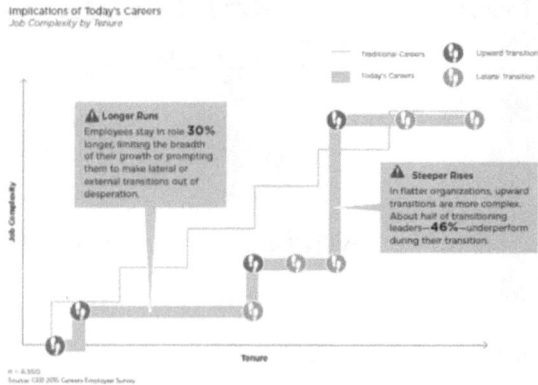

When promotions occur, employees often take on significantly more complex responsibilities, resulting in traumatic transitions because they are unprepared.

In addition, the lack of movement and staying longer in their roles means they often fail to get a broad range of development opportunities they need to perform effectively in more senior positions resulting in the wrong and inefficient lateral movements.

Growth-Based Career Culture

So then, the question is, how could I effectively move and grow in an organization? Before answering that question, let's see what growth means and if it differs from development because people usually mix the meaning of career growth or progression with career development, but they are not the same.

When we talk about career development, we refer to acquiring skills or becoming more proficient in a competency. To do that, organizations usually use Individual Development Plans (IDP) to document the skills and activities that will support your development in one to two years. However, one year is the most common practice in the traditional model. So, people assume that because they acquired specific knowledge and skills, experiences, exposure, and accumulated time, it is time for a promotion, which is incorrect.

We need to understand that career growth is a bigger picture. The conversations around career growth usually involve the possibility of performing different roles, taking other responsibilities, or enhancing the scope of their position, which will take longer than the approach in career development. Also, other aspects are involved, such as behaviors, judgment, capability, etc.

What is experience-based career growth?

Shifting to a more agile, flexible, and realistic career approach that responds better to multiple generations' aspirations focusing on skills development and strengthening competencies instead of positions or promotion timelines, implicates identifying the best employee experiences.

Remember that experience is the vehicle to obtain the skills or competencies, not the mean. To define a successful career model based on experiences, we must consider balancing organizational, individual, and industry needs. Also, it requires active participation and ownership of business leaders, building trust and partnership with the employees supported by technologies that will be the enablers. In the following image, you can see an example of a holistic approach

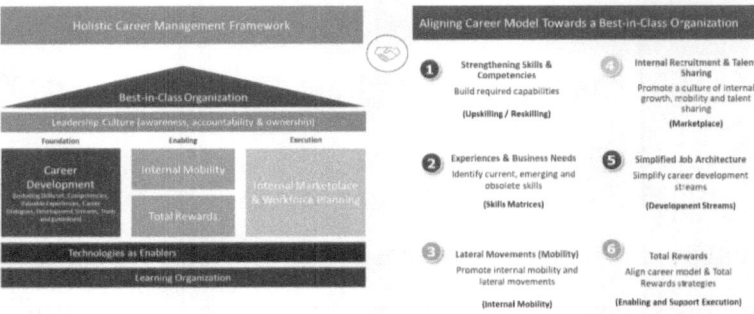

The experience-based growth approach is embedded into the Career Development piece of the previous framework. It consists of identifying skills and areas of expertise required at different organizational levels based on the expected contribution.

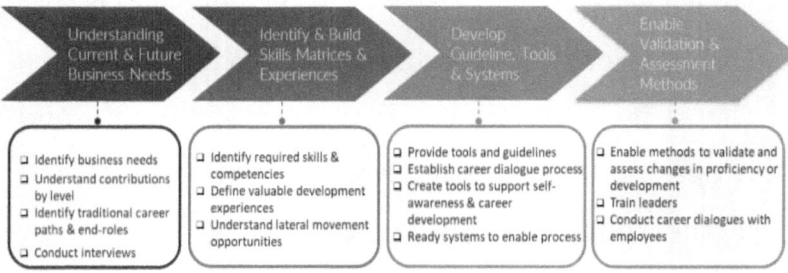

Then persons in partnership with their leaders agree on which experiences could better support the person's development and align with the person's interests, goals, and capabilities.

Growth-based vs. Promotion-based

In the traditional models, growth refers to your organization's ladder or career lattice, as it is called in more modern environments. The main difference is that the ladder usually considers only the vertical movement in the organizational hierarchy, while the lattices consider vertical and lateral movements.

Therefore, we could say that a lattice is more closely related to the approach of the experience-based growth model in its concept. However, it will depend on the approach because the drivers could be different in the case that follows the promotion-based approach, which in most companies refers to the time in positions.

Another form to refer to possible moves a person could make within the organization is called career paths. Career paths can be designed using ladders or lattices. Also, they could be more static or dynamic depending on the approach we decide on as part of our career framework strategy.

Usually, career paths are thought and designed around jobs and responsibilities, trying to go deeper than lattice in the detail of the progression routes. Career paths generally follow the promotion-based approach with predefined positions to follow.

We can use career paths in a growth-based approach, but the difference is that the definitions are around skills and areas of expertise required at each organizational layer instead of around jobs. The career paths could be represented in multiple forms and career models.

Independently of the career model you are using, the career paths must be used to give the person clarity, transparency, and certainty with a realistic approach.

Promotion-based is founded on climbing the latter, so it is mainly vertical. Usually, people exposed to this model frequently get frustrated because they feel they are the next in line. So, promotions and development depend totally on the vacancies, budget, and years in the position to be considered for the next move.

In the following image, Gartner clearly shows the difference between Promotion-based and Growth-based.

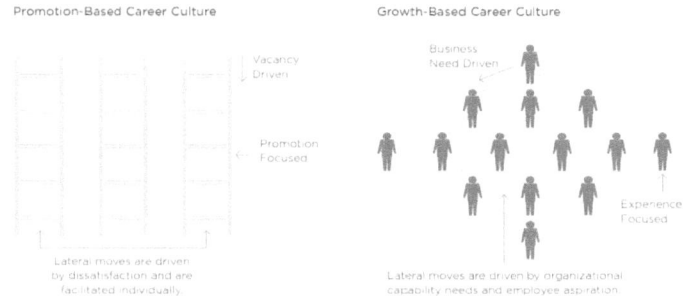

Transforming a Promotion-based career into an Experience-based

Now that we understand the difference let's find out how to transform a traditional promotion-based career into an experience-based one. Below is an example of a general manufacturing career map based on positions and the time a person needs to be at each level.

I will use this example to explain how you can transform your career maps into an experience-based growth approach.

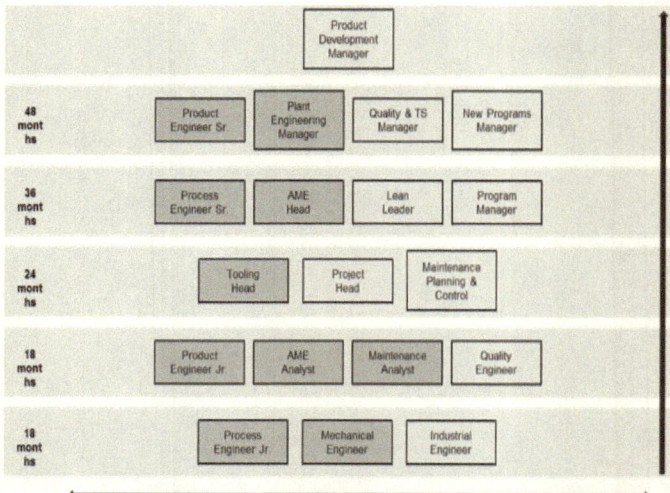

As explained in the previous section, a promotion-based career model indicates the time you need to stay at each position and a predefined sequence of positions you must go through to progress in your career. Therefore, I highlighted some positions to simulate possible career paths following that approach.

When we see or design something like this where the positions are mapped, our first thought is that they should be there for a reason. So, the first logical question I should ask is why those positions were mapped there. Next, I need to understand what skills or experiences a person should gain at each step of that ladder. By knowing that, we know the mapped positions' intention ("Why") and the critical skills a person should acquire in each position.

Next, we need to continue hacking the career map to find out the application of that. In other words, what the person is expected to do with that knowledge and experience and how they will successfully gain the necessary proficiency to progress in their career.

During this analysis, you will discover that not all the boxes are necessary. However, in some of them, the person must partially understand that role to continue progressing in their career, so they could be transitory.

To help you convert your traditional career model from a Promotion-based career approach into an Experience-based career, you can use the following questions presented by Gartner in one of their studies:

- What contributions are expected at each level?
- To succeed in that role, which capabilities do people need to be advanced or master?
- In which roles or assignments do people gain those capabilities?
- How can people develop those capabilities?

When analyzing the career maps in the promotion-based approach, you need to have a clear picture of the starting and ending positions to decide when defining the experiences and areas of expertise.

Growth-Based Career Culture

As I mentioned, you will discover that some positions do not add much but are still there, or just a few skills are gained at that position overall. Also, start identifying areas of expertise, then you can narrow the long list of skills to start building your skills inventory focused on critical areas and knowledge.

Remember that the experiences are the vehicle, not the mean.

Here are some examples of possible experiences that you can use.

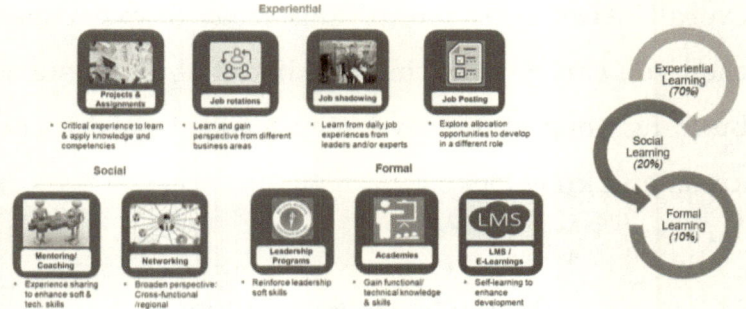

Overall, this approach will provide learning experiences, lateral mobility, and resources to persons aligning their interests with business needs. In addition, we will help employees excel in their current job and prepare them for the future with learning, development, and advancement opportunities. Finally, we will promote and develop a partnership culture in the organization.

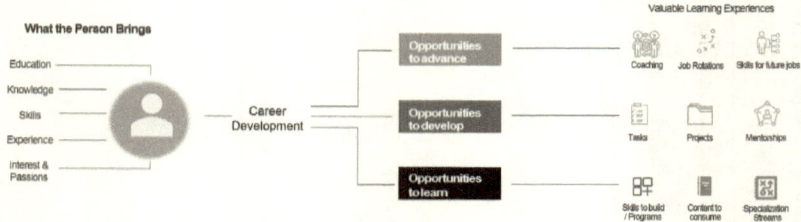

How and Where to Start

When we start working, we usually do not dedicate time to thinking about a development plan. Occasionally, we do not even have clarity on the types of work we can do in the organization. Also, many organizations do not have robust onboarding plans, so you start doing stuff when you arrive.

To break that, you must work on your development plan from the beginning and socialize it with your leader to have another point of view, develop a partnership, and align expectations. Learning about the culture and building networks in the first months could be the difference between success and failure in the long run.

In this chapter, I will share some models I implemented based on my learning experiences. I saw a difference in my team members when they paused, reflected, and planned their careers as part of their main activities. In this section, you will find what I implemented with my team and observed that gave us positive results, as well as what happened when a team member didn't understand the value of learning the culture and building networks at the beginning. That is more important than starting to have meetings or doing any task.

One of the biggest mistakes we make when we arrive at a new organization is trying to demonstrate from the first minute that we can add value, losing the opportunity to learn. I observed many people who do not take the time to understand the environment and explore their growth opportunities.

When I once hired a new Global Manager, she never understood the importance of dedicating the first month to learning the culture and building networks with her peers in other countries. Instead, she was so anxious about doing something that she made mistakes, got in conflict with her team, and lost the opportunity to establish networks with other countries. Instead, she focused on what she considered the "power" of her position when that role worked by influencing others, collaborating, and partnering with other regional teams.

I spoke a couple of times with her to explain the importance of that and to slow down to build a strong starting line, but she told me that it didn't match with her previous experiences where on day 1, she had a busy agenda attending meetings.

Her anxiety level was so high that after a couple of weeks, she talked with my boss and asked him to speak to me to follow her mental approach. I will not tell you the end of that story because you can imagine how it ended. When she left the organization, her team was relieved and thanked me for the decision. But ultimately, she did not understand how to start and affected her team with just a couple of months in the position.

Surprisingly, the other team members, including the guy who left the position, expressed that they would wish to have that time when they arrived at the company. Also, the feedback from the regional groups was that she never understood how to work with them, and obviously, they avoid interacting with her.

So, this is just an example of how important it is to plan our development plan and decide where we should start when we arrive at an organization to not fail as that person did.

This example demonstrates that you can fail even with a high capability but not the right behaviors. You can review the following table to decide and plan your development. Remember that it is just one of the multiple options you can choose, but we observed it works pretty well as a general framework for people in functional and technical areas. The table gives some recommendations to you on what you could focus on to elaborate your personal plan.

a) For people in functional roles

		GET STARTED	
	Year 1	Year 2 - 4	Year 5+
FUNCTIONAL	Get to know the culture and potential pitfalls	Strengthening core and leadership competencies connecting with company values and explore mentoring	Sponsor talent development and explore becoming mentor
	Understand Company's operations and industry	Gain Business Acumen / Cross-functional	Connect with business strategies to enhance competitiveness and business performance
	Start building your networking	Expand your network with other functions, regions and/or customers	Nurture relationships with local industry, stakeholders and/or communities
	Seek Career Dialogues with your manager/direct reports	Conduct Career Dialogues with your manager/direct reports	Conduct Career Dialogues with your manager/direct reports
	Understand expected contribution & require experiences of your role	Seek out new experiences to develop current and future skills and knowledge	Keep abreast on your function Seek career diversification

Growth-Based Career Culture

b) For people in technical roles

	GET STARTED		
	Year 1	Year 2 - 4	Year 5+
TECHNICAL	Get to know the culture and potential pitfalls	Strengthening core competencies connecting with company values and explore mentoring	Share your knowledge by becoming a mentor
	Understand Company's operations and industry	Gain deeper knowledge in company's processes and technical competencies	Focus on your leadership / supervisory skills and competencies development
	Start your networking	Expand your network with other functions, regions and/or customers	Have a clear understanding of global technical trends for business transformation
	Conduct Career Dialogues with your manager/direct reports	Continue with Career Dialogues with your manager/direct reports	Continue with Career Dialogues with your manager/direct reports
	Understand expected contribution & require experiences of your role	Get focus on technical specialization according to your aspirations and role	Enhance expertise gaining depth in technical experiences/challenges

Both tables are pretty much the same, with slight differences. Until now, I mentioned stuff related to your development. But what about if we put it into a broader perspective of a career journey. Then the following table can help you.

MY CAREER JOURNEY					
KNOW MYSELF	EXPLORE POSSIBILITIES		PLAN FORWARD	MAKE IT HAPPEN	
1. My Career	2. Career Dialogue	3. Development Areas	4. My Career Plan	5. Experiences Execution	6. Evaluation & Follow-Up
1.1 Learn about Career Mgmt philosophy	2.1 Explore interests and aspirations with my Manager	3.1 Explore required experiences, knowledge, competencies and skills	4.1 Learn about development opportunities offered (Learning, Mentoring, LMS, etc.)	5.1 Apply defined experiences in daily job to enhance my development	6.1 Validate acquired experiences, knowledge and skills
1.2 Focalize development according to my experience & tenure	Align expectations with business context and job application	3.2 Identify areas of interests with type of related work	4.2 Define my Career Plan with development actions and job application	5.2 Monitor my progress	Conduct follow-up Career Dialogue with my Manager to plan next actions

As we explained, there are multiple models to manage careers in organizations. Therefore, I suggest you dedicate some time to learning about the learning culture in your organization. In step 2 of the table, the career dialogues are critical and shouldn't be too structured. Try to agree on a time to discuss your plan and aspirations. In some cases, you need to find a space to talk with the Manager once Removed (MoR – it is the Leader of your Leader) because it can add an additional perspective and support since there is no conflict due to the hierarchical distance.

To help you develop your Development plan (step 4.2), I design a four-step method to guide you. Follow these steps to define your Career Plan according to the experiences you would like to acquire to enhance your potential and development.

1. My Career Goal - Focus on specific goals
o What are you willing to reinforce or strengthen in the short (1-2 yrs.) / mid (3-4 yrs.) / long term (+5 years)?

2. Experiences / Capabilities I need to leverage
o Identify based on your Self-Reflection the areas in which you would like to focus your development
o What is required to achieve that goal? What gaps do you need to close?
o To be successful focus on the most critical, not more than 2-3 to be reinforced

3. Identify Development Actions & Job Application
o Commit and partner with your Leader in development actions that will support closing your current gaps.
o Define how you will apply the experiences in your daily job, the expected duration, and who will validate its accomplishment

4. Document in Individual Development Plan (IDP)
o To keep focus and track your agreed development actions, be sure to document them in your IDP

Finally, defining where to start will depend on a certain way on where we are in our careers. But remember that this connects with your capability.

Growth-Based Career Culture

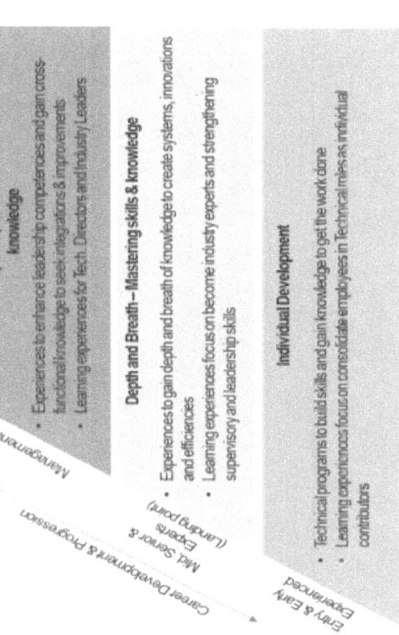

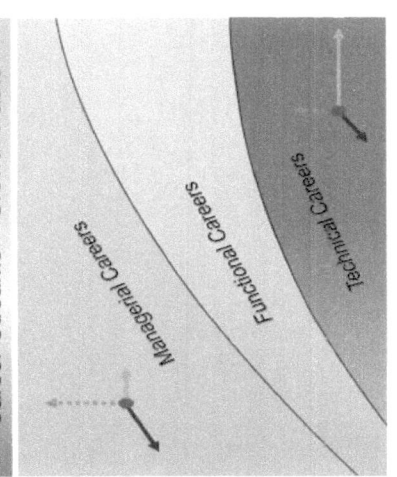

Employees need to apply and practice the knowledge to gain the experience and expertise that will help them to move ahead in their careers

To master technical skills, employees must apply knowledge and practice to gain experience and expertise. The time to transition is related to the time to master the skill rather than the role

CHAPTER 5

UNLEASH YOUR POTENTIAL

We need to consider and understand some things to unleash our potential. One of the first things is that every Human Being is born with a particular capability, and we can't go beyond that because it is part of our DNA.

Unless we get genetically modified, our human capability will grow at a certain pace and up to a certain level. There is a method to track our human capability's evolution using a tool Elliott Jaques designed called the Potential Progression Curves. That model helps us to project in curves the progression of our capability through the years.

Our human capability is part of our nature and can't be changed, but it will progress no matter what we do. Our capability enables us to deal with the complexity of situations and demonstrate our potential. In other words, when we apply our human capability to solve a problem or make a decision, we are demonstrating our potential.

To understand better, we can divide our capability into two parts, the maximum capability versus the applied capability. The maximum capability is part of our nature and can not be observed in day-to-day activities. Then the applied capability is what people usually see in our daily behaviors, decisions, etc.

The gap between our maximum capability and the applied capability is called Potential. So, since the applied capability is nurtured, we can work on it to reach our maximum capability. This connects with the definition of work that we will explain in the next chapter. Remember that our applied capability relates to our behaviors, decision-making process, problem-solving skills, and judgment. There are two more concepts that you need to understand in your journey to unleash your potential. Those are the Time-Span and the Four Absolutes.

Time Span

The Time Span of discretion is the scientific method Elliott Jaques discovered to measure the complexity of work. The Time Span is the measure used to understand the complexity of any task by understanding how long it takes to accomplish it. With the Time Span also, we can observe the effectiveness of a person when performing a task.

Elliott Jaques defined the Time Span in his book "Time Span Handbook" as the length of time a person can effectively work into the future without direction, using their own discretionary judgment to achieve a specific goal.

By understanding this and putting it into an honest introspective, we can identify which tasks we are usually more effective in and how long in the future our decisions were about. Then it is just a matter of looking for the right challenges that match our capability to be in flow and continue growing.

One mistake we make is to believe that high-level positions will help us unleash our potential, which is not necessarily true because if we do not have the capability required for the role, we will be a big failure. It is a fact that when the complexity is higher than our human capability, we will feel overwhelmed and be working long hours because we will not be in flow.

The Four Absolutes

The four absolutes will help us understand what is essential to succeed in any role, regardless of the function or level.

To succeed in our careers, we need to have all of them, but the most important is the first one, which is capability. If we do not have the capability required, then the others don't matter.

So, the four absolutes are the following:

1. Capability (Time Span)
2. Skills
    a. Technical Knowledge
    b. Practice
3. Interests and Passions (value)
4. Reasonable Behaviors
    a. Habits
    b. Culture
    c. Minus T Behaviors

As we mentioned, the capability will allow us to deal with the complexity of the tasks, connect the dots correctly and help seek good experiences.

The second absolute is about skills, we could have the capability, but if we do not master our skills, we can not effectively demonstrate our potential and apply our capability. So, gaining knowledge and practice are crucial too. There is a magic number of hours used in the industry to consider that someone is an expert, and that number is 10,000 hours of consistent practice.

The third absolutes are very important and connect with work-life balance and the big resignation, which are interests and passions. If we do not become interested in what we need to do, we will make our minimum effort, and our commitment will be very low. But, on the other hand, if we have low interest and passion, we will not develop or show our skills and capability entirely or at their maximum level. So, interest and passion value what we do and are entirely related to our engagement level.

The fourth absolute is our behaviors, including our habits, how we fit into a culture, and the out layer behaviors of our temperament. In terms of culture, we could have all the first three absolutes previously described, even good behaviors, but if we can not commit to the culture, we will fail because we will not fit in.

Let me give you an example of this. After interviewing many good candidates, finally, you have your ideal candidate. You were careful to ask what you consider the right questions about the capability, skills (knowledge and practices), interest, and passion, so the person looks to be the right one in alignment with the nature of the work.

Now, did you check its habits and behaviors? Because for example, if the person can not commit to the work schedule or the uniform that s/he needs to wear, they will not fit in and eventually fail or have too many problems until they leave. Remember, the person needs to fit with all four absolutes. So, I am sure that you remember someone in that case, and honestly, it could work in a short time, but the reality is that it will not work for both of you (person and employer) in the long run. In other words, your interest and passions are your compasses, the skills are your toolset to do the work, your capability is your mindset, and the behaviors are the part that feeds your commitment and discretionary effort. All of these will determine how you will interact with others. So I suggest you self-reflect on your four absolutes when planning your next move or development.

Right learning experiences

When looking for the right learning experiences, you must consider that you must work on your Mindset, Skillset, Toolset, and Behaviors. Specifically, critical behaviors because many great professionals failed or derailed their development and careers because they did not work on particular behaviors and habits.

Remember, people get hired because of their skills and knowledge but get fired because of their behaviors and habits. When looking for the right learning experiences, that process requires a conscious and honest exercise of introspection to guide our development decisions. Do not try to get shortcuts because you will pay the price later in your career. Instead, take the time and patience to mature at each stage of your development and take advantage of lateral opportunities. Those will help you be more rounded and solid later in your career.

Some people get focused on escalating the corporate ladder as fast as possible, but I can tell you that speed in your early stages will cost you more when you are up there if you don't mature enough in your skills and behaviors. As one boss told me, remember that what brings you here is not necessarily what will get you there, referring to the top positions in my function.

Many people are not patient enough to appreciate lateral career movement. In my experience, the people that invest in lateral movement at some point "recover" the time invested and reach faster Senior level positions where they succeed more.

Almost all the C-levels I know dedicate time to their development by moving laterally or even to another area. Of course, many high-potential programs have that characteristic too.

Follow your Passions Wisely

To follow your passions wisely, you need to be honest with yourself and be realistic about your aspirations in the context of your capability to align your potential with your interests. The best way to explain this is by sharing a team member's story who always told me he wanted to be a director whenever we discussed his career development and interest. So, there is nothing wrong with that. But, in fact, you could be a director in one company and not necessarily you could be a director in another or have the same success that you had before. It will depend on the complexity of the work and whether you are in flow with it.

Returning to the story, the issue with my team member was that he didn't reflect on his gaps. Consequently, he didn't accept or work on acquiring the right skills required for the work that ambition, even when he struggles to deal with the complexity of his current job, which affects his objectivity, resulting in missing opportunities to develop.

He was so obsessed that he didn't notice that his interaction was always based on his technical expertise. He was our guru but was not appreciated by senior team members at the next level of responsibility. So, this is an example of how being disconnected from our reality could make you lose valuable learning experiences. So, instead of pushing, it may be better to try lateral movements to give him another perspective on his aspiration.

Another example of this is my personal experience. I was never aware of these things I am talking about until I went up in my career and learned about these concepts that helped me be conscious of my journey. That allowed me to do back engineering of my career progression. Then, I understood why I wanted to be the expert in my area of expertise at the beginning of my career. Little by little, my interests changed.

I can tell you now that I am not interested anymore in being a guru. In fact, that has very low value for me at this point in my life. Instead, I am more passionate about transformation and how my experiences could help others or give my two cents to improve our society and HR practices.

That is what I mean when I say follow your passions wisely because that implicates to be constantly thinking about your drivers and fears and re-aligning your strengths to continue growing.

Of course, some people say you need to unlearn to do that, but again it is not about skills; it is about being in flow and adapting your knowledge and aspirations to new scenarios and realities to achieve your goals.

Back Engineering to Unleash Potential

If we understand our human capability and how it has evolved over the years, we can do a back engineering exercise to make better decisions to maximize our potential. So, it is essential to reflect on the purpose of your development and then think about which learning experiences and knowledge could help you grow.

For example, suppose you are at the beginning of your career. In that case, you may be involved in activities associated with producing something compared to another person with more years of experience interested in defining systems, methods, or using best practices. So, after some years, you have gained more experience and learned how to do the job and use good practices related to your function, and now you are expanding your scope and vision.

Now that you have become an expert, it is time to decide which path to follow, so you can continue gaining more depth or breadth of knowledge or explore to start a managerial journey. When transitioning from expert to something else, you need to self-reflect and think about what makes you happier. In my experience, we do not take this moment to stop and connect with ourselves to validate if we are going on the right track.

Usually, we are too focused on "growing" by getting our new job or promotion that we do not notice that, in some cases, we made the wrong turn, making us feel that we failed or unhappy.

If that is your case, you can stop and make a U-turn. But you must understand your drivers and what makes you happy because that is the natural human way to connect and validate your capability versus the complexity of whatever you are doing. If you feel overwhelmed with what you are doing, maybe the complexity of what you are doing exceeds your capacity, which is fine. There is nothing wrong with accepting that. On the contrary, accepting it will make you feel a release and better if you dare to be honest with yourself.

If you feel bored or overcomplicating stuff around you, maybe that indicates that you can deal with something more complex. Then is the time to think about that as well.

In the next chapter, I will cover the future of work and the importance of connecting with what makes us happy as one of the key elements to dealing with the new normality.

Back engineering on our life decisions will help us to be happy in the future.

CHAPTER 6

THE EVOLUTION OF WORK

What is Work now and in the Future?

To think about the future of work, we must first understand what work is about. We can refer to work as solving problems and making decisions over time.

To perform a job, we need to use our capability, which is part of our DNA and cannot be changed. We can potentiate our capability in different ways to achieve our maximum capability. Also, different types of work require different capabilities. So, it will be interesting to reflect on the future of work in terms of its nature and understand the possible evolution of human beings and their behaviors.

Later in this chapter, we will connect these ideas with the nature of the work that artificial intelligence (AI) can perform. Understanding the nature of AI and distinguishing between complexity and complication will be essential.

In McKinsey's study titled "What is the Future of Work" mentioned: "The future of work is one of the hottest topics, with conflicting information from various experts leaving plenty of room for debate around what impact automation technology like artificial intelligence (AI) and robotics will have on jobs, skills, and wages."

In the study, they referred to another article published in December 2017 titled "Jobs Lost, Jobs Gained: Workforce Transitions in a Time of Automation," which mentioned: "Automation is not a new phenomenon, and fears about its transformation of the workplace and effects on employment date back centuries, even before the Industrial Revolution in the 18th and 19th centuries."

The Evolution of Work

In the 1960s, US President Lyndon Johnson empaneled a "National Commission on Technology, Automation, and Economic Progress."

Among its conclusions was "the basic fact that technology destroys jobs, but not work." In my opinion, technology does not destroy jobs either but speeds up their evolution supporting humans with repetitive duties and bringing the opportunity to add value differently.

The mindset shift is more about finding how to add value instead of performing activities. However, new technologies go beyond just performing repetitive activities; they work based on sophisticated algorithms that create the impression that they are thinking.

For example, some people say that AI algorithms learn and robots think. But is that really true? Or are they just choosing from billions of options following a very advanced logic embedded in their algorithms with an advanced binary tree of decisions?

The thinking process involves many factors, such as experiences, conscience, values, emotions, feelings, and judgments that AI has not yet. This is relevant to consider when we think about the future of work and how new technologies influence the transformation of work.

We can refer to a study published by Deloitte where mentioned: "The future of work is being shaped by two powerful forces: The growing adoption of artificial intelligence in the workplace, and the expansion of the workforce to include both on and off-balance-sheet talent. So what changes could be in store for the workplace, the workforce, and the nature of work itself?"

So, they are saying that we need to have the capability to understand and incorporate technologies to deal with the complexity and add value by combining both. AI has its own nature, which mainly adds value in the first two strata, where its nature is more related to the kind of work that AI or Robots are contributing.

The International Labour Organization (ILO) addressed the future of work in what they called "The Global Dialogue." This explores and exanimates the future of work to better understand the drivers of the current changes, such as technological innovation, the changes in the organization of work and production, globalization, climate change, the regulatory environment, and demographic and migration shifts. This aligns with what we previously mentioned and how the new generation will interact in this new environment that will continue evolving.

New Generations and the Future of Work

It is essential to mention that the future of work is not only related to new generations. The organizations have been talking and worried about the new generations for many years, but maybe only a few could be proud of their achievements related to this topic. The new environments demand a better balance between generations and interests.

When we talk about New Generations, it is crucial to reflect on the effectiveness of the management in the organizations and evaluate how they are dealing with this challenge. So why do I mention the leaders? Because management and leaders in the organizations are the cornerstones of all these.

For years, I observed that many organizations relayed their efforts on superficial aspects such as furniture, food, colors, etc., and forgot to work on the mindset shift of their leaders, resulting in failure initiates. On the other hand, suppose an organization wants to succeed in engaging new generations so in that case, it will need to work with the leaders to inspire people regardless of the generation. Then it will be part of the culture.

As much literature mentions, great leaders are the ones that inspire people with their passion. Some leaders respect and value people, treating them as the most critical element of the company. Others focus on controlling the activities of the team.

As my friend, Tom said, "some leaders think that being a leader is to put in place a reporting protocol where people must report to them their activities, but the purpose of the reporting lines is more than report activities to someone else."

Mediocre leaders are worried about operational and financial indicators or who will report to whom. Unfortunately, those types of leaders are the ones that destroy organizations because they cannot build the culture that the company will need to address in the future, so they are just juggling the present.

As the former CEO of Magna, Don Walker, once said in an interview published in 2012, "You need to treat your employees like customers."

Today, different generations interact in organizations, and the new generations have a great opportunity to drive the future of work with the support of other generations. So, they need to inspire the generations that will not have the passion or the energy to deal with the fast changes we observe in the work environment.

Therefore, it is necessary to consider a mix of visions and passions in this new world to find the right organizational balance for the future. In addition, some people related to previous generations will face the last stage of their careers, and their needs and passions will differ from those starting or in the middle of their journey.

According to the OECD, this aspect is crucial to consider when we imagine the future of work since life expectancy is increasing. Shortly, the average life expectancy in the world will be 84.3 years old for men and 86.6 years old for women.

Other aspects of considering are that new generations like the post-Z generation or generation Alpha have recently been unofficially called the "Gen C" for the impact of Covid in their lives. Gen Alpha is highly influenced by technology and purpose, so the effect of the pandemic will somehow redefine who they are in the new normality.

Gen Alpha is growing up looking and learning from the behaviors of the millennials. They will have the opportunity to learn from what worked and what didn't, including the aspirational or more idealistic part but now also with the life experience of the pandemic.

They and the new generations will shape the new conditions that demand organizations evolve again. If we can say that millennials disrupted the status quo of the organizations, then the generations after are the ones that really will evolve how we work today.

If we guide Gen Alpha properly, they will be the generation that will change the world because they have been exposed to many changes and global situations that will make them see the world from a different angle and purpose. Generation Z and Alpha have lived more things affecting the world than most of us. They learn to live in the pandemic with limited access to their friends and relatives, they observe how their parents, or a close friend got unemploy, they got exposed to many different social problems, etc. Inclusively, they learned faster and better about the home office and how to learn in virtual environments. They adjusted their social skills faster to better prepare for the future.

Now, the challenge is that all those situations will require organizations to think differently and creatively when those people are collaborating with them. So, yes, you read it well; I say collaborating instead of working because most will look for different ways of working. But not only will new generations impact the future of work, but there are also other aspects that we need to consider when we think about the future of work, such as immigration, changes in demographics, people with better education, social and political changes, including the possibility of the colonization of other planets in the near future.

The ILO addresses many of those aspects related to the future of work in at least a fourth conversation:

The first conversation is focused on work and society, asking questions such as: How does the nature of work affect the coherence of our communities? How is work diversified and undertaken in different settings, and what are the economic consequences and the potential impact on our society?

The second conversation focused on the nature and creation of jobs.

The third conversation concerns the organization of work and production, and

The fourth conversation deals with the governance of work.

There are important questions to be answered, as Lord Robert Skidelsky addressed in his keynote speech in Geneva at the ILO event in April 2017. His speech focused on two main questions that I take literally from the ILO report:

(i) How will the meaning of work and leisure evolve with technological changes? And

(ii) How will working time be affected by technology

and other drivers?

If you want to learn more about these points and others, read the document published by the International Labour Organization (ILO) called "The Future of Work We Want: A global dialogue," there, you can read in detail about these essential points.

In his report, the ILO addressed another critical question: "how to shape the future of work for youth?" This question is fully connected with this section since we mentioned at the beginning that people need to be happy and look for jobs that help them fulfill that purpose. So, even considering that we can't generalize due to the vast diversity of youth-related elements, we can mention that new generations would have different perspectives and aspirations of workers. Moreover, as the document noted, younger generations may not have the exact linear job expectations as prior generations. According to that document, the norm today is to have several short-term jobs, including unpaid and volunteer work and internships, with limited social protection.

I observed that young people have a higher social consciousness. Their desire and courage to change things at different levels of organizations and society go beyond what older people generally demonstrate. For example, they are usually more involved in politics, solving social inequalities and environmental issues than previous generations. Another aspect is that stability and safety have a different meaning for younger generations than for Baby Boomers, Gen X, or other contemporary generations. This is changing since most organizations were designed for those generations.

In the same way, if we connect these with careers, the career models in the organizations should evolve to models based on providing experiences to the people putting the skills in the center rather than setting predefined paths of positions or defining timelines that indicate the time to progress in your career.

Additionally, governments need to modernize their educational models and reinforce the civic values that will support the evolution of societies.

The big resignation is challenging what we thought would be the way to add value to our employees. Also, it demonstrates to the organizations that people are not tied to a paycheck and are willing to make sacrifices.

In consequence, the corporates need to rethink their positions and be more generous with the people because now the people are unwilling to continue in that unfair and unbalanced situation. Many people have decided to quit their jobs partly because the pandemic demonstrated that it is possible to have a different balance in the working relationships but also for a social effect where people ask for and deserve a better balance in all aspects of their lives. So people are no longer willing to have that feeling of sacrificing their lives and families for a job or company. In that regard, some organizations are reasonably trying to respond and adapt to the new reality. However, others are still trying to force their employees to return to the past working mode, which is now obsolete and will not be accepted by the new generations.

The Evolition of Work

In the following years, the organization will need to deal also with Quiet Quitting, which will impact the organization more in the workforce and skills needed, culture, and organizational climate. If you don't know about Quiet Quitting, it refers to doing the minimum requirements of one's job and putting in no more time, effort, or enthusiasm than is absolutely necessary.

What is an augmented workforce?

The augmented workforce is the combination of human beings and technologies working on work together. So, why is this relevant? As many studies mentioned, as of today, there is practically any job that can be automated at 100%, so the opportunity relies on how we can maximize both capabilities. Therefore, artificial intelligence and other technologies will play an important role in the evolution of work. Thus, with the incorporation of technologies, other changes and challenges arise, and the aspirations of the persons evolve, which is the case of career advancement.

In the future, people will not be appreciated for how many hours they invest or if they are physically at the office because technologies will make that obsolete and more costly to produce or interact with. However, some organizations have started realizing a new way to ensure high performance and automate the process using different technologies. The augmented workforce will enable a new way to work at a different time without physical presence at the workplace, where flexibility in performing the work will be more important than hours worked towards high performance.

In this journey, some leaders will need to challenge their paradigms, more in manufacturing, regarding the men-hours per piece, long working shifts, or physical presence to do the job. Also, more hours do not necessarily mean more productivity, better performance, or commitment. As we learned with the levels of work, sometimes working more hours could be a red flag showing misalignments between the complexity of work and the person's capability.

The Work-Life-Balance

Work-Life-Balance is not new, but I observe that having a purpose and feeling that we are in balance without the sense that we are in a trade-off is gaining more importance among people regardless of the generations. Moreover, being aligned with our passions and interests is very important nowadays.

I consider that the pandemic helped us better appreciate the moments we live with the persons that matter to us and see more clearly. But unfortunately, in some cases, we were so immersed in our professional lives that we forgot to enjoy those moments.

I feel that people need to make a hard stop at some point to re-evaluate what matters most and seek the right conditions for that. If something can kill the feeling of having a balance in your life is when you feel that to obtain something, you must sacrifice other aspects of your life. That is too bad because, at some point, you will feel guilty or regretful of your decision. So, remember that the time can't come again to give you another opportunity to live it again.

Being in alignment with your interest and passions will help you to identify your purpose better and keep the focus on what makes you happy. I never knew anyone doing something that passionate and complaining about their work. We learned when we were kids that sometimes we need to make sacrifices to obtain something better, but I do not feel we should continue thinking that way.

Sacrifice implicates losing something, so why should we want to lose something? Instead, we must consider reflecting on our purpose, interests, and passions and understand that we must put in the effort, commitment, and perseverance. When that becomes scarify, we need to re-evaluate if that is realistic or maybe it is too ambitious for that moment in time. I am not saying that you just drop the ball and stop, but I suggest breaking the goal into small pieces that allow you to continue enjoying and keeping in balance.

The Work in 2030 and Beyond

Think about how the work will be in 2030 and beyond sounds like a science fiction topic today, but it is not too far. According to an article published by Business Insider, we could see that and more soon if we consider that NASA plans to send humans to Mars in the 2030s.

These make it inevitable to start thinking about jobs in that context. But we must also consider what skills we will need for those days. How should the leadership models and theories evolve to be accurate and relevant to deal with the challenge of cohabitating in different worlds? Maybe now sounds crazy, but how many years do you expect that to happen? At some point, we should consider that at the beginning, the colonies will need to find a way to survive and establish an efficient way to make life sustainable. But what will happen after that? Will they see the Human Beings 1.0 as inferiors?

The interplanetary organizations, at some point, will need to communicate and interact with the organizations on Earth, so we will need to evolve and be prepared for those interactions. It is a possibility that new societies will be practically isolated from other colonies or individuals. Maybe they will be working more in their places, making face-to-face interaction less frequent or unnecessary, affecting those individual behaviors changing in different ways. This is why I consider that current models will not fit in that context. Imagine that Humans in outer space will be like Cavemen reloaded because they will have access to advanced technologies with better and faster connections. Maybe they will replicate some of what we know from our ancestors. It is possible that resources may not be present in abundance, so people will try to make everything efficient, so companies will need to find new forms to provide more dynamic and extended work environments. Another question will be how to connect the different Worlds, considering that we succeed in achieving a sustainable way of living on other planets and on Earth. I think the balance between People and organizations will turn around so that the organizations will be around individuals and societies. In other words, Organizations will need to find a way to access the people, not the other way around, as it happens nowadays.

Assuming we can send people to other planets, would humans from outside Earth will see humans on Earth as less evolved? Will they understand work as we know it today? Or will it be the beginning of the transformation of the work as we know it right now? Well, I think it is too early to conclude anything, but it will be true that the best and worst of our species' customs and practices would flourish as has happened throughout history.

Based on McKinsey's study, it would be jobs that can be automated through 2030 and jobs that may be created in the same period. Therefore, we must be prepared and evolve our capabilities to address the near-future challenges. Having an open dialogue to shape the future allows us to align everyone's interests to address the near future challenges and drive our evolution.

CHAPTER 7

THE NEW NORMAL & THE GREAT RESIGNATION IN THE WORLD

Finding your Place in the New Realities

In December 2019, a new pandemic (Covid-19) started in the world in China. It was the beginning of a new reality for human beings, not only in how we interact with each other's but also in all aspects of our lives.

The labor opportunities were impacted drastically. The traditional forms and styles of the past didn't respond appropriately to the new challenge. So, if the world changed that much, how can we balance my aspirations and happiness with the new reality if we see that people are losing their jobs and uncertainty is part of this new reality?

The good news is that this situation will become the new normality, so people will start finding new opportunities and jobs. Remember that this type of challenge brings new opportunities. So you can see this as a big problem or an excellent opportunity to reinvent yourself and reflect on your next move.

Finding our place in the new reality will implicate reflecting on our priorities, fears, and strengths and acquiring new skills and behaviors. We need to think about work and society differently.

The Big Resignation in the World

Nowadays, Big Resignation is a phenomenon that is impacting the world. The pandemic makes people think about how they have to live and the conditions of their jobs.

With the pandemic, people had the opportunity to make a hard stop and rebalance their priorities, in some cases because they lost their jobs, but in others, because the circumstances and lockdowns forced people to stay home. From one day to another, the whole world must learn how to live this new reality and make adjustments, but also the pandemic caused visible the huge inequity that many people face daily.

Now, when we look forward, the Big Resignation is not just a matter of rebalancing our lives but also dignifying what we do. Today, more than ever, dignity and balance are related to productivity, and work is not about how many hours we invest in something. Instead, work is about understanding that many people are unwilling to continue sacrificing their lives for a salary. Instead, they value the time spent on what makes them happy. This shift in the work also impacts society and its values, and hopefully, it will help in the evolution of Human Beings.

Remote work is also making some people move to their original hometowns, and that is also impacting the economies on different scales. Also, the Big Resignation brings opportunities for immigration which is part of the history of humanity.

Immigration also affects other aspects like education, culture, housing, health, and work. Therefore, when a group of immigrants moves massively to a country, the place that will receive them needs to prepare and consider many factors that, with a poor response, could generate significant problems for the community at the same time that will help in the evolution of the society and the working conditions.

So, Big Resignation is a complex matter that Organizations, Governments, Societies, and Universities should tackle together. Since the pandemic, around 4.0

to 5.0 million people have quit their jobs for different reasons, and the number is still growing, so the challenge is immense.

What is Coming Next

Since I can't predict the future, I hope organizations, governments, and people find a way to balance their interests and motivations. Organizations must understand that forcing people to return to their offices is going nowhere. In fact, it will bring them more negative impacts than the short-term benefit of having someone in their buildings.

The effect on their reputation will be something new generations will not forget, and they will be the less desired organizations where new generations will look to work. Of course, the situation in developing countries would be different, but at some point, they will be impacted by a similar reality.

If the organizations are unwilling to be less greedy and offer a more equal environment, people will continue to leave. The traditional work environment based on having people in a building will disappear in the next few years. It is probed that remote work has enormous benefits for everyone and, in many cases, is more productive.

Artificial Intelligence (A.I.), Augmented Workforce, Industry 5.0, and other technologies and social aspects will make this revolution happen in the production lines that, at some point, will catch up with other areas of this revolution too.

It is a reality that the world will continue evolving. For good or bad, the A.I. is moving very fast in different directions and aspects of our lives. ChatGPT and other tools can do unimaginable things you could not even imagine one year ago.

Nowadays, it is hard to identify if you are interacting with a real human or an algorithm, so we need to be prepared to adapt ourselves and be open to the new world coming today.

ACKNOWLEDGMENT

It took me almost three years to write this book. But, as an amateur writer, I feel very proud because it could not be possible without the support and friendship of many amazing people who accompanied me on this journey.

I am very grateful to everyone who taught me something or challenged my thoughts. So, this time it is my turn to thank you again because somehow, each of you influenced my life for good.

I would like to thank my friends, Julia, Rolf, and Marcos, for helping me understand concepts such as Level of Work, and Human Capability, among other exciting topics. It was amazing and a privilege to learn from you guys.

To Tom, my traveling companion through Europe and Asia. He showed me how to quickly and practically explain the definition of work and "Time Span." to managers and executives. I also enjoyed the fantastic stories that he shared during our trips.

I want to express my appreciation to someone who sees Career Development differently. So, thank Julie for helping me see and talk about Career Development from a different perspective aligning career aspirations with opportunities, and thinking about what I want to DO, not BE. That way of thinking inspired one part of this book. So, thank you for deciding not to be an elevator operator in your Grandparents' store.

Also, thank you to my teams and colleagues who challenged and supported me in transforming the HR function. All of you helped me to better understand how new generations perceive and expect the future of work.

One has been here for years among the people who helped me grow. He is one of the most generous people that I have met in my life. He inspires me about how we can impact and influence societies and organizations and help others be prepared with audacity for the future. So, thank you, Lotfi "compadre," for being my friend and teaching me many things professionally and personally.

Finally, and the most special one, I would like to thank my parents, who worked hard to give me the best education, guide me in life, and encourage me to have dreams and work to achieve them. They always have been close to me and for me at any time. I love you so much!

ABOUT THE AUTHOR

Roberto is an international practitioner with more than 20 years of international experience in the Private sector and Multilateral organizations in America, Europe, and Asia. He worked in multicultural environments, presenting his ideas and leading global solutions that helped companies transform their HR function. Roberto has participated as a speaker and panelist in different forums in Mexico, the USA, and London. He holds a bachelor's degree in Electronic System Engineering and an MBA from the Technological of Monterrey. He also participated in an Executive Development Program at Stanford University School of Business. His professional aspiration is to influence other HR practitioners to provoke and generate wellness in society that sparks better life conditions for human beings. He believes we need to start disrupting the markets to write a new story that responds better to the organization's future needs and people's aspirations.

www.ingramcontent.com/pod-product-compliance
Lightning Source LLC
Chambersburg PA
CBHW020659220526
45464CB00001B/501